6/16/04 To Loures,

Hope you enjoy the
book. and if it inspires
hope)

Charlie Derber

D1505429

REGIME CHANGE BEGINS AT HOME

CHARLES DERBER

REGIME CHANGE BEGINS AT HOME

FREEING AMERICA FROM CORPORATE RULE

BK

BERRETT-KOEHLER PUBLISHERS, INC.
San Francisco

Copyright © 2004 by Charles Derber. All rights reserved. No part of this
publication may be reproduced, distributed, or transmitted in any form
or by any means, including photocopying, recording, or other electronic
or mechanical methods, without the prior written permission of the
publisher, except in the case of brief quotations embodied in critical
reviews and certain other noncommercial uses permitted by copyright
law. For permission requests, write to the publisher, addressed
"Attention: Permissions Coordinator," at the address below.

BERRETT-KOEHLER PUBLISHERS, INC.
235 Montgomery Street, Suite 650 San Francisco, CA 94104-2916
TEL: 415-288-0260 FAX: 415-362-2512 www.bkconnection.com

ORDERING INFORMATION
QUANTITY SALES Special discounts are available on quantity purchases
by corporations, associations, and others. For details, contact the
"Special Sales Department" at the Berrett-Koehler address above.
INDIVIDUAL SALES Berrett-Koehler publications are available through
most bookstores. They can also be ordered direct from Berrett-Koehler:
TEL: 800-929-2929; FAX: 802-864-7626; www.bkconnection.com
ORDERS FOR COLLEGE TEXTBOOK/COURSE ADOPTION USE
Please contact Berrett-Koehler: TEL: 800-929-2929; FAX: 802-864-7626.
ORDERS BY U.S. TRADE BOOKSTORES AND WHOLESALERS
Please contact Publishers Group West, 1700 Fourth Street,
Berkeley, CA 94710. TEL: 510-528-1444; FAX: 510-528-3444.

Berrett-Koehler and the BK logo are registered
trademarks of Berrett-Koehler Publishers, Inc.

Printed in the United States of America

Berrett-Koehler books are printed on long-lasting acid-free paper.
When it is available, we choose paper that has been manufactured by
environmentally responsible processes. These may include using trees
grown in sustainable forests, incorporating recycled paper, minimizing
chlorine in bleaching, or recycling the energy produced at the paper mill.

Library of Congress Cataloging-in-Publication Data
Derber, Charles.
    Regime change begins at home : freeing America from corporate rule /
by Charles Derber.
        p. cm.
    Includes bibliographical references and index.
    ISBN 1-57675-292-5
        1. Business and politics—United States. 2. Corporate power—United States.
    3. United States—Politics and government—2001– I. Title.

JK467.D47 2004
320.973—dc22

2004041056

FIRST EDITION
08 07 06 05 04   10 9 8 7 6 5 4 3 2 1

Produced by Wilsted & Taylor Publishing Services
    Production management by Christine Taylor
    Copyediting by Rachel Bernstein
    Design and composition by Jeff Clark

TO ELENA

for lighting the spark

CONTENTS

ACKNOWLEDGMENTS

Without Steve Piersanti, the publisher of Berrett-Koehler, this book would not have come into being. Steve is a brilliant editor who helped me reframe this book into a coherent argument and went way beyond the call of duty, supporting me at every stage and giving me his time on holidays, on workdays, and late at night. Steve is also the founder of Berrett-Koehler, the best publishing house an author can work with. A huge thank you to Steve, and all of you wonderful folks at BK Publishers, for your tremendous talent, help, and support.

Many thanks also to Ralph Nader, Ted Nace, David Korten, Yale Magrass, John Naar, Wayne Rifer, and others who took the time to read and comment on the manuscript. And thank you to Dan Wasserman for the gift of your cartoons.

Special thanks to John Williamson and David Karp. John helped me come up with the idea for this book and supported me all along the way with his characteristic humor, intellectual insight, and good spirits. David took the time to read multiple drafts of chapters, gave me inspired commentary, and was always there with his inimitable wit and humanity.

And finally, I want to thank Elena Kolesnikova, who, among other things, helped bring electricity to this project. She saw how this book could look before I could see it. Elena is a gifted writer in her own right, and where there was a flaw in the conceptualization or a need for a spicy phrase or major reorganization, Elena saw it and helped fix the problem. Thank you, my dear Elena, for being so talented and so generous. As you well know, I couldn't have written this book without your creativity and long hours of inspired labor on the chapters. You lit up each page as you light up my life.

What we need now is not just a regime change in Saddam Hussein and Iraq, but we need a regime change in the United States.[1] JOHN KERRY

INTRODUCTION

WHEN BAD REGIMES HAPPEN TO GOOD PEOPLE

MEET DAVID BILLINGSLY

David is a forty-six-year-old certified accountant with an MBA and a CMA. He got his degrees in the late 1970s and early 1980s and found a good job with a midsize, growing company. He got married, had two kids, and bought a house. He had a good bonus plan and pension program. He was living the American Dream.

Ten years into the job, David was laid off. He found a job at a major computer corporation after several months, but six years later, the firm started to lay off full-time employees and hire outside contractors. He was out of work again, but this time "I was prepared, I had my job search. Have vita, will travel."

But now it was the recession of the early 1990s. With his savings dwindling, David started taking temping assignments in accounting at one-fourth of his former salary. After years of part-time, temporary, and short-time permanent jobs, even after his wife got a job, he explains, "Now it's survival. It's putting food on the table. When my roof starts to leak, what do I do? The hot water heater goes, I don't have the five hundred or thousand. I can't buy a car and the brakes are going. My wife and I, our teeth are rotting away, and we don't have any dental insurance."

David feels he's being "double raped" by the companies and the temping agencies that bill for $20 and give him $11. As the manufacturing jobs melt away, he says, "We screwed up, we're going down. Like the Romans or the Egyptians or the British, we're on the decline." The politicians are out for themselves, David believes, and both political parties are in bed with the corporations. He voted for Ross Perot in the 1990s and doesn't vote anymore.

David doesn't see a future now. "I'll tell you how bad it is: I've got a copy of Derek Humphrey's book on suicide. I want to be prepared because I don't believe that I'll ever work on a stable basis again."

David's words echo the stories of many Americans I have interviewed over recent years.[2] Although no two are alike, they are all experiences of people on the verge of despair, betrayed by the very institution that was to deliver their dreams—the American corporation. For these people, the

American job—the rock on which the American middle class was created—had turned into what David calls a "one-night stand."

How sad, you might think. But should these poor souls —as cruel as it sounds—be written off as unfortunate but necessary victims of "business as usual"? Or worse yet, could they simply be, well, losers?

The Americans I interviewed have been downsized, outsourced, reduced to temping, freelancing, and part-timing. But this rapidly swelling pool of workers is no longer a statistical shrug-off. Together they now represent *one-third* of the American workforce.[3] Furthermore, along with millions of other hardworking folks in this country, they have done everything right—the American way. They worked long hours, educated themselves, were creative and loyal. It was the system—or what I call the *regime*—that step-by-step turned against them.

But let us look beyond the workplace. If we pull ourselves for a minute out of our collective trance, we'll see that the current regime is actually rigged against all of us. Whether, like David, you are struggling to make ends meet, or your livelihood is in no immediate danger, you, too, are a casualty of today's regime!

THE REGIME AND YOU

You may drive an SUV, enjoy a bigger house and higher household income than you expected, have four televisions and two really cool flat-screen computers. But think about your credit card debt. Or how long and hard you work (a month longer, on average, than most Europeans). And look around. Your local public schools and libraries are underfunded and probably rotting, your health care costs are spiraling, your tap water may not be safe, your state's roads and bridges are deteriorating and may not be safe for that SUV (which might roll over on you anyway). There's more. American unions are busted. Our tax system is skewed, robbing Peter to pay the very wealthy Paul. Our elections are manipulated (think Florida) and constitutional rights compromised (think Patriot Act). Big money drowns out your voice in Washington, D.C.

How can we go about building the American Dream if the principles of the common good and of democracy, the very foundations of this glorious country, are being dismantled before our eyes, brick by brick? And as we let our government bang nail after nail into the coffin of our dreams, how can we explain why all this is happening today in the United States?

WHEN BAD REGIMES HAPPEN TO GOOD PEOPLE

I argue in this book that all is not doom and gloom: this perversity can be explained and changed. Here is my premise: Americans are good people with strong democratic traditions. The problem lies in today's regime—a system of rule based on underlying, and now deeply worrisome, imbalances of power in society between money and people.

Central to the current regime is corporate ascendancy, a balance of power tipped in favor of corporate elites who have succeeded in parlaying their financial clout into the greatest hostile takeover ever: the acquisition of Washington, D.C. These brazen corporate raiders have enforced their political will by taking away from us, the public, our constitutionally endorsed authority. We have seen big business wield political influence before, but never have we had trillion-dollar transnational corporations gain such overwhelming control over our nation's beautiful capital, and over all of America itself. Today's corporate regime is unique, and uniquely dangerous.

Conceived in the 1970s and shaped by the election of President Ronald Reagan in 1980, the current corporate regime has been steadily consolidating power. The result so far: profits grow and democracy shrinks. George W. Bush has pushed the envelope, taking the regime in more extreme directions as Washington becomes a money swamp, and people like you and me have too many days when we feel helpless to change it.

Behind the ostensible government sits enthroned an invisible government owing no allegiance and acknowledging no responsibility to the people. To destroy this invisible government, to befoul the unholy alliance between corrupt business and corrupt politics, is the first task of the statesmanship of the day.[4]

PRESIDENT TEDDY ROOSEVELT

> *There is an evil which ought to be guarded against. . . . The power of all corporations ought to be limited. . . . The growing wealth acquired by them never fails to be a source of abuses.*[5]
>
> JAMES MADISON,
> *author of the*
> U.S. *Constitution*

The American system wasn't supposed to work this way. The Founders crafted the Constitution to ensure that "We, the People" would have a voice in our own affairs—and in those of the nation. The Constitution embraced an elaborate set of checks and balances that were to separate government agencies and prevent concentration of power. The Founders realized that checks and balances apply to corporations.

In today's regime, giants such as Wal-Mart, GE, and Merrill Lynch have accomplished what the Founding Fathers most feared. They have hollowed out the institutions that enable ordinary Americans to have a say in how our land is governed. To cover up this hijacking of our constitutional and democratic rights, the regime has targeted you and me with a classy Madison Avenue arsenal of manipulation techniques—from democratic rhetoric to downright deception. Think just about the bald lies recently constructed to justify war against Iraq, a war that brings back spooky memories of Vietnam.

HAVE YOU THOUGHT ABOUT REGIME CHANGE AT HOME?

After 9/11, President Bush declared regime change to be official U.S. policy. He took this country to war to create regime change in Iraq. How does the president know which governments to overthrow? According to Bush's criteria, a government must

build or sell weapons of mass destruction
violate U.N. resolutions
threaten, invade, or dominate its neighbors
exploit many of its own poorest citizens
erode the civil liberties or human rights of its people
fail to live up to democratic ideals

The president, of course, was thinking of countries like Iraq, Iran, North Korea, or Syria. But look at the list more carefully. Sound familiar? The criteria that call for regime change apply to the American government itself.

Americans live under a regime that is threatening to dominate not just its neighbors but the world as a whole. Did you know that the U.S. government is the planet's biggest producer and merchandiser of weapons of mass destruction and that it has voted against and violated hundreds of U.N. resolutions?[6] It treats our poor and many of our workers, such as David, in ways that violate U.N. conventions. It is violating our most important civil liberties and our own highest democratic ideals. It is eroding hope, not just in workers such as David Billingsly, but in millions of other Americans.

I was one of the hundreds of thousands of Americans who went out into the street to protest against the war in Iraq. While I was walking on the streets during one protest, I glimpsed—among the hundreds of colorful signs denouncing the war—a poster that made a different statement. It said, simply, "Regime change begins at home." The clever twist made me chuckle. But as I reflected on it, the idea struck me as profoundly serious. I argue in this book that you should take it seriously too.

Many Americans do not agree with the president's policy of regime change abroad. Who is the United States to decide the fate of foreign governments? How can the United States violate international law and preemptively strike against governments that have not attacked us? If regime change became the policy of other governments, wouldn't the world descend into chaos? But regime change at home is a policy that all Americans can—and should—embrace.

Regime change at home doesn't threaten other countries. It does not violate international law and it doesn't create prospects of chaos in the world. It will not breed anti-Americanism or more Islamic terrorism. And it certainly does not violate the American Constitution or any American laws or values.

Regime change at home is the highest form of American democracy. Instead of preemptive war, it is proactive citizenship. It is the form of American politics blessed by the American Constitution. Some of our finest moments in American history have come from prior regime changes at home—and when you get involved personally, it can be one of the most meaningful parts of your own life. And here's another plus: when we succeed in regime change here, we set a model for citizens in other countries who need their own regime change.

Regime change at home isn't easy, partly because the ruling regime has not only made us disposable but also taken away our hope. Many of us believe our troubles can't or won't be fixed, and we have little faith that getting together and organizing with other workers or citizens can make a difference. No wonder that David Billingsly finds himself considering suicide. The regime has killed his belief in the possibility of change itself.

Although I understand David's despair, I show in this book that there is strong reason for hope. No earlier American regime has survived for much more than a generation, and this one will not be any different. *True, short-term developments—including the frightful possibility of George W.'s reelection in 2004—could boost the current regime, but these cannot stem the longer-term conditions that doom the current regime.* So be hopeful, but be aware of what is killing off hope in David, and perhaps in you, too.

Part of our loss of hope involves the loss of choice in Washington. American regimes are systems of power that transcend particular administrations and parties. The current American regime has enlisted all presidents since 1980 and has swallowed up both political parties, including the majority of congressional Democrats. While there is deep partisan bitterness between Republicans and Democrats, both are more concerned with staying in power and serving the big monied interests that put them there.

This is not the same as saying there are no meaningful differences between the parties. The Democratic base, which opposed the war in Iraq and is angry about big busi-

PARTY DRINKERS BEWARE

When I told my students at Boston College about this book, they begged me to call it *Bush Lite*. Since they are students who enjoy a few glasses of beer after class, I could understand their passion for the title. In truth, it conveys one of the key insights about U.S. corporate regimes: that they erode democracy by turning many elections into a choice between a party of big business and a party of big business with a softer voice. While our current corporate regime is more closely identified with the Republicans than with the Democrats, much of the Democratic Party establishment is Bush Lite. While it bitterly fights Republican control, it drinks from the same tap of big money and tastes, to the average citizen, just a little smoother.

ness domination of Washington, sees the world differently than the Democratic Leadership Council (DLC), the mainstream voice of the Democratic Party leadership, as well as the Republican establishment. Moreover, even the Democratic Party establishment differs in important ways from the Bush Republicans. The Bush administration is the radical frontier of the corporate regime, and its foreign and domestic policies are more extreme than those of other regime voices, including DLC Democrats and even those of Bush's own father.

But a call for regime change at home is not just an argument against President Bush and the current congressional leadership. (I focus in this book on the presidency, but the same arguments apply to Congress.) Beating Bush in 2004 would grievously wound the regime and might begin to turn our lives around in small ways, but it would not equal regime change. Regime change goes beyond changing a president, a party, the congressional leadership, or even electoral politics itself, requiring basic change in institutions and culture. Regimes change only with underlying tectonic shifts in social power and with the rise of new social movements. Nonetheless, defeating particular presidents—or the rule of a particular party—can be essential to the politics of regime change. Bush is such a president, because he is the corporate regime's most extreme face, a symbol that can potentially spark the grassroots movements that make politics relevant to workers like David.

WHY REGIME CHANGE
SHOULD MATTER TO YOU

One aim of my book is to help make you smile about our nation's sad state of affairs. But mainly I want to persuade you of a strategy of how to achieve regime change, including how to approach 2004, and how to move the country in a new direction in the long term, regardless of who wins the elections. Here is my road map:

PART I I tell the histories of corporate regimes in the
United States and how they have been toppled in
the past.

PART II I spotlight the Bush administration as a window
into the extremism of the current corporate regime,
showing the damage it has done to the country and
why it must resort to wars of deception to survive.

PART III I lay out a vision and strategy for regime change at home over the long haul.

Let me briefly indicate how my argument is essential to readers from many groups—from liberals to conservatives to populists—and why we should all come together to change the current regime. My main hope and challenge is to inspire you and unite citizens of many different persuasions to reclaim the country from the elite that has hijacked our government.

ANYBODY BUT BUSH

You may belong to the group that I call Anybody but Bush (ABB), a group that includes most partisan Democrats, many progressive or leftist radicals disaffected with the Democratic Party, some Independents, and even a few Republicans. If you are an ABB person, you see Bush as so dangerous that your only concern is beating him, even if it means electing a conservative Democrat who is Bush Lite. You are looking for the strategy that will defeat Bush; my argument is that this is intimately linked to longer-term regime change, and that those of you who are ABB must focus not just on Bush but also on the regime he represents.

The 2004 election is really about the survival of the corporate regime and what direction the country will and should go in the twenty-first century. We are not likely to defeat Bush and change the country without understanding the larger significance of the elections; *we need a vision of a twenty-first-century alternative to the current regime.*

ABB people must recognize that the Democratic Party, because of its current stake in the regime, will have difficulty gaining the people's support until it begins to speak out against the corporate regime and embraces a new vision. If you are ABB, you need to know the historical evidence that shows Democrats win when they don't simply mimic Republicans in sheep's clothes. I shall review this evidence throughout the book, but one need only look at the emotion and electoral support won by former Minnesota Senator Paul Wellstone, precisely because he spoke so passionately for a real alternative.

HELLO, ALL DEMOCRATS

I hope to persuade members of the Democratic Party itself—including congressional politicians—and the liberal base of a related argument. A Bush victory in 2004, combined with a GOP sweep of the Senate and the House, would be a catastrophe for the Democratic Party as well as the country. The Democratic Party has been split between the Establishment Camp, who are Bush Lite, and the Base Camp (the strongly partisan grassroots Democrats), who are disaffected and want real change. Regime change highlights an old question that plagued the Democrats in two former eras dominated by big business: the Gilded Age and the Roaring Twenties. In both periods, the Democratic Party became a copycat of the Republicans and almost made itself extinct, electing no presidents in either period with the exception of Grover Cleveland, a parallel to Bill Clinton today. The Democrats are running that risk again.

If the Democratic Party does not wake up and fight for regime change, social movements will push it aside and offer the country another voice for the people.

NO-SHOW VOTERS

I hope to show why regime change matters to readers who are part of the electorate in general, and are disaffected by both parties or unclear about how or whether to vote in 2004 or successive elections. Many of you already understand that both parties currently speak in different accents for the same regime and reward the giant global corporations that fund the candidates at the expense of the voters. Since you already distrust both parties, you are among 100 million people (one out of two adult Americans) who are likely nonvoters and disposed to tune out politics unless you hear someone speaking honestly about the crises affecting your life. Only the politics of regime change can make politics relevant again for you and help you deal with the urgent problems of your life and communities. While older voters may be skeptical, a large number of the disaffected are young people who have not voted but are hungry for new ideas and a new politics. Candidates who capture disaffected voters like you will prevail in 2004 and beyond, and regime change politics has the best potential to turn you from a couch potato into an engaged citizen.

TRADITIONAL CONSERVATIVES

Conservatives are surprisingly ripe for the kind of regime change that I discuss, and I think the ideas here will resonate with you. Traditional conservatives abhor concentrated power, whether in big government or in big corporations. I know from my own extensive experience talking to libertarians, small business proprietors, and other conservatives on AM radio talk shows that a critique of the corporate order resonates with many of you. The current regime, being a marriage of big business and big government, is the antithesis of the capitalism that traditional conservatives embrace. Nor do corporate globalization and American empire appeal to many of you, who see it as the work of high finance with no loyalty to anything but money. As mentioned earlier, the gap between neoconservatism and traditional conservatism is huge, and many former Republicans, such as former Nixon advisor Pat Buchanan or the best-selling writer and strategist of the "new Republican majority," Kevin Phillips, see the neo-cons as hijacking their own heritage.[7] Bush is popular among social conservatives who care about abortion, gun control, and taxes, but there is a big opening in the conservative world for a challenge to the global corporate system, and winning a large group of you over is key to regime change.

RADICALS

Progressive, populist, or leftist radicals, your structural critique is essential to the regime change we need, and I hope to show you how important your role is today. Regime change is systemic and arises out of grassroots social movements that are visionary enough to reject the regimes of their eras and capture the imagination of the public with an alternative. Radicals are the heroes of regime change politics, but many are disenchanted with electoral politics and have lost hope in the Democratic Party as a tool of change. My effort here is not to persuade those of you who are radicals to suit up with the Democrats or to take attention away from your work in communities, but to help you think about the relationship of your own vision to the politics of regime change. Neoconservative radicals took this task seriously in the 1970s and succeeded.

At minimum, radicals today seeking to topple the current system of global corporate power need to understand and appreciate your monumental role in earlier regime change. From ousting Union Jack to desegregating our schools and lunch counters, social movements ought to be credited for the finest moments in U.S. history:

18TH CENTURY Movement for independence
19TH CENTURY Abolitionism
1880S AND 1890S Rise of populism
1910S Suffragist movement
1930S Unionism
1960S Civil rights movement

Social movements—not mainstream parties or third party candidates—are always the ultimate architects of regime change. Today, populist movements rising among labor, environmentalists, women, minorities, peace activists, and religious communities can help propel the nation and the Democratic Party beyond the current crumbling corporate regime. If a new Democratic president, such as

John Kerry, is elected in 2004, the movements will be critical in determining whether he pastes a cosmetic gloss on the current regime or moves to help create a real democratic alternative.

SKEPTICS AND PRAGMATISTS

My biggest challenge is convincing skeptics who don't believe in the possibility of regime change. Skeptics may be fatalists who don't trust they can make a difference or "pragmatists" who see regime change as utopian, believing either that there never has been *de facto* regime change in American politics or that the end of history has arrived and the pendulum will never swing again. Well, you make a good point. The current regime does have a more powerful hold on power than did earlier ones:

It has uniquely deep hooks in both mainstream political
parties.
It has unprecedented control of the mass media and
the exceptional power of new electronic media to
indoctrinate the population.
It has been effective in eroding countervailing power,
particularly unions.
Ordinary citizens are now more dependent than ever
on corporations for jobs, pensions, information,
entertainment, health care, and almost every sphere
of daily life.

Doubts about change are well-founded and cannot be ignored. But sitting still is no alternative. The regime is facing serious stresses that could create regime change quickly, and skeptics should find this argument interesting, if only because it will change your reading of the American experience into one in which significant realignment periodically occurs. I will show that regime change is the stuff of American politics, and it has been a permanent dimension of U.S. history from the Revolution to Ronald Reagan. While regime changes in the United States are not usually revolutions, they reflect periodic deep-seated shifts in the values and direction of the country.

Regimes tend to be so strongly constructed that their change always seems utopian. That is the purpose of regime ideology: to persuade you that things must always be the way that the current regime dictates. Regime change means rebuilding all of the regime elements, and it requires imagination and hope. But toppling a system that violates its own national creed may be easier than you think. United, we can do it. And then we can remember all over again why America is such a great country.

PART I

The Corporate Regime

When American leaders talk about regimes, it is usually about the evil governments of Iraq, North Korea, Iran, Syria, or Cuba. As U.S. power brokers see it, a regime is a horrible government somewhere else in the world that the American public ought to distrust. Regime change, by the same logic, is about how the United States can rid the planet—as it claims it did in Iraq—of a government that it views as a threat to civilization.

The dictionary defines a regime as "a manner, method, or system of rule or government." If we take this literal approach and view any "system of rule" as a regime, then the U.S. government is also a regime, and the history of the United States—as of other nations—can be seen as a succession of regimes. American regimes, I argue, are entrenched systems of power and ideology. Regime changes at home, while not revolutions, are great dramas, creating seismic shifts in power and social values. Regime changes are political earthquakes that deeply affect the personal lives of ordinary Americans and can steal power away from the people—or return it to them.

Our current regime is a corporate one, and I start by describing what a corporate regime is and how it has subverted our democracy. This is the third corporate regime in American history and, while more global and hazardous than its predecessors, it is not entirely new. Its roots lie in the Gilded Age of John D. Rockefeller, who helped shape the first corporate regime, and in the Roaring Twenties of Warren Harding, Calvin Coolidge, and Herbert Hoover, the leaders who presided over the second corporate regime. I tell the story of each of these regimes and how they have cumulatively contributed to the crisis in our nation today.

Fortunately, corporate regimes have not been the only forms of rule in America. Both the first and second corporate regimes ended in regime changes led by progressive and New Deal movements. The systems of rule turned power back toward the people.

Today, more than ever, we need regime change at home, better than the ones before. To achieve it, we need to understand how brave, earlier generations of Americans toppled the corporate regimes of their day. Regime changes do happen in America and, sometimes, they light up our lives.

CHAPTER 1

THE SINS OF THE REGIME

Regime" has a nasty ring to it. We hear about Saddam Hussein's regime, the North Korean regime, Fidel Castro's Communist regime, the radical clerical Iranian regime, or the Syrian dictatorial regime. You get the idea. A foreign government that is repressive, and that U.S. leaders would like to see eliminated, will get branded in the United States as a "regime."

That is why the idea of an "American regime" seems so strange to Americans, who have been conditioned to think of regimes as bad governments somewhere else. Have *you* ever imagined the term can be applied at home? Maybe not, but the dictionary makes clear that the term applies to any "system of rule," at home or abroad. Europeans, Africans, Latin Americans, Middle Easterners, and Asians

Certificate of Birth

Name: Third Corporate Regime

Date of Birth: Election Day, 1980

Father: Ronald Reagan

Mother: Corporate America

Headquarters: Washington, D.C.

Current Caretaker: George W. Bush

Brief Biography

The regime is twenty-five years old.
It took form under the Reagan administration. The regime consolidated itself
under Bush I, secured legitimacy from
Democrats under President Clinton, and
radicalized itself under Bush II. The aim
of the regime is to shift sovereignty
from citizens to transnational corporations, and to transform government into
a business partner committed to maximizing global profits for a small number
of global executives and shareholders.
It is showing signs of age and is viewed
by much of the world as dangerous.
Caution is advised.

Registry of Regimes, Washington, D.C.

talk frequently about the "American regime," which they fear and mistrust.

Regimes are institutionalized systems of power, good or bad, that rule a nation. Every regime is like a political house built around five great pillars. The pillars usually support the ruling elites, but in democratic regimes they can empower the people. The architecture of the house and the design of its pillars reflect the underlying balance of power in society. The groups or organizations that control money tend to design and run the "house."

MEET THE PILLARS

1) **A dominant institution** (e.g., the corporation, the government, the church) that ultimately controls the house
2) **A mode of politics** (e.g., corporate sovereignty, theocracy, representative democracy) that determines how the house is run
3) **A social contract** (e.g., the welfare state, laissez-faire, libertarianism) that sets the terms for the tenants
4) **A foreign policy** (e.g., isolationism, empire, multilateralism) that dictates the relationship to the neighbors
5) **An ideology** (e.g., social Darwinism, socialism, individualism, democracy) that spells out the creed of the household

President Bush is the United States's most recent and extreme regime leader. He has done some expensive renovation of the pillars, in collaboration with the big monied interests that helped put him in office. He has changed the façade of the regime but not its underlying structure or aims.

WHO IS GEORGE W. BUSH?

Let's be clear: Bush should not be treated as a power unto himself. He is simply the most militant custodian of a regime that preceded him and will likely persist after he is sent back to Texas. Nonetheless, regime change looms because of Bush's extremism and the underlying terminal cracks in today's aging regime.

Regimes cling to power, claiming that God or nature has ordained them. A nineteenth-century regime leader, John D. Rockefeller, said, "The growth of a large business is merely a survival of the fittest . . . the working-out of a law of nature and a law of God."[1] This sort of rhetoric is popular in the current regime, with neoconservative ideologues from the Reagan to the Bush administration portraying the American "free market" system as part of nature, and corporate capitalism as the highest stage of social evolution. One of the regime's favored thinkers, Francis Fukuyama, a former Reagan administration official and now professor of public policy at George Mason University, calls the current American order "the end of history," evidently God's and man's most perfect creation.[2] But while the new corporate regime is deeply entrenched and controls the public conversation, it has not ended history, which in the United States consists of a never ending contest between the existing regime and those seeking regime change. America's first ruling elite was the British colonial authority, a victim of the most dramatic politics of regime change in the nation's history: the Revolution. Under George Washington's first presidency, a Hamiltonian business regime warred with and ultimately triumphed over Jeffersonian Republicanism, to be followed by a succession of new regime changes.

A BRIEF HISTORY OF U.S. REGIMES

U.S. REGIMES

First Corporate Regime
Built by the robber barons 1865–1901

Progressive Regime
Led by trust-busting President Teddy Roosevelt 1901–21

Second Corporate Regime
Brought to you by Presidents Warren Harding and Herbert Hoover 1921–33

New Deal Regime
Designed by President Franklin Roosevelt 1933–80

Third Corporate Regime
Sponsored by global corporations and Presidents Ronald Reagan, George Bush, Sr., Bill Clinton, and George W. Bush 1980–????

While you won't read about regimes in most history books, American history is a series of fascinating regimes and regime changes. The modern history of U.S. regimes began immediately after the Civil War, when the earliest American corporate regime was born. Art Garfunkel sang *"Don't know much about history,"* but if you want to understand the current regime and how it uses power against you, you have to know its history.

THE FIRST CORPORATE AND THE PROGRESSIVE REGIMES

The *first* corporate regime was born with a bang after the Civil War. John D. Rockefeller, J. P. Morgan, and other robber barons built America's first great national corporations in one of the world's most impressive bursts of economic dynamism and abuse of power. The regime developed as a marriage between the robber barons and the presidents of the era. Republican presidents Grant, Harrison, Garfield, Arthur, and McKinley and Democrat Grover Cleveland all carried water for the new captains of industry. The robber barons dominated American society from the end of the Civil War until 1901.

Sound familiar? The parallels between this first corporate regime and the one today are haunting. The late-nineteenth-century robber baron regime created many of the historic companies, such as Chase National Bank (now J. P. Morgan Chase), First National Bank and National City Banks of New York (now Citigroup), Standard Oil (now called Exxon), and U.S. Steel (now called USX), which, after various mergers, still dominate America. It was the first regime to flood politics with corporate money and create all-powerful corporate lobbies in Washington. Rockefeller's aides, with briefcases literally stuffed with greenbacks, worked in the offices of senators' who wrote legislation on oil, banking, and other industries. It's no secret why they were called "robber barons." They used their influence over presidents to send in troops when workers tried to organize, and they helped write tax laws that created a huge and growing gap between the very rich and everyone else. We live in a born-again robber baron regime, with the corporations bigger and more global, and their domination of Washington even greater.

Despite its awesome power, this first corporate regime faced a radical challenge by the Populists, fiery farmers and plain-spoken people from the heartland who created the People's Party in 1892, captured the Democratic Party in 1896, and launched one of the country's most important politics of regime change. They proclaimed in 1892 that corporations were being used "to enslave and impoverish the people. Corporate feudality has taken the place of chattel slavery."[4] While the Populists melted away with the 1896 presidential defeat of their candidate, William Jennings Bryan, they helped give rise to the reform movement of the Progressive Era under the

> *Like earlier invading hosts arriving from the hills, the steppes or the sea, [the robber barons] overran all the existing institutions which buttress society, taking control of the political government, of the School, the Press, the Church, and . . . the world of opinions or of the people.*[3]
>
> MATTHEW JOSEPHSON,
> *The Robber Barons*

"trust-buster," President Theodore Roosevelt. In 1907, Roosevelt called for "the effective and thorough-going supervision by the National Government of all the operations of the big interstate business concerns," a direct challenge to the "free market" regime discourse of the robber barons. Roosevelt was no revolutionary, but he did engineer his own regime change politics, culminating in his effort to create a Bureau of Corporations that would put limits on the strongest Rockefeller, Morgan, and other robber baron fiefdoms. Corporations had to restructure themselves and embrace a measure of public accountability, as the Progressive Era consolidated political power in a new regulatory regime quite different from the robber baron order. The eminent historian of the Progressive Era, Gabriel Kolko, labeled the resulting government-led regime "political capitalism." The Gilded Age corporate regime passed into oblivion.[5]

THE SECOND CORPORATE REGIME AND THE NEW DEAL

The Bush administration resembles not just the Gilded Age presidencies but also the Republican presidencies of the 1920s, which presided over the nation's *second* corporate regime. The Harding, Coolidge, and Hoover administrations abandoned the regulatory impulse of the Progressive regime and turned Washington back to big business. While less constitutionally extreme than the Gilded Age presidents, they created a regime of corporate hyperpower, dominated by an ideology of corporate self-regulation and paternalism. They proclaimed a union-free world known as *Plan America,* a vision of corporate paternalism in which big business would house and educate workers and provide them with medical care and retirement. Plan America was a vision of a whole society wrapped in a benign corporate cocoon, without need for government regulation or unions, previewing some of the views about corporate responsibility fashionable in the current regime. President Hoover said that the government "owes nothing" to himself or any citizen, since the business world had created opportunity for everyone and could police itself. The Roaring Twenties saw an era of overwhelming corporate dominance enlivened by booming prosperity, scandals such as Teapot Dome, and a huge stock market bubble that popped in 1929. The regime ended with market collapse and the victory of President Franklin Roosevelt in 1932.[6]

Spurred by the Depresssion and the recognition that capitalism could be saved only under a different order, Roosevelt created the New Deal, a regime that established basic rights for labor, codified in the Wagner Act, and created an entirely new social welfare system built around Social Security. The New Deal did not end corporate power, but it turned the government into a limited agent of countervailing power and sought to preserve a public sphere, whether in the health system or in the post office, safe from corporate predators. Economist John Kenneth Galbraith wrote at the height of the New Deal that the federal government's main peacetime role is to rein in corporate power, a statement that no established thinker or politician could have entertained in the Gilded Age or Roaring Twenties regime.

THE GREATEST
AMERICAN REGIME

The New Deal regime was the longest and most important in modern American history. It lasted several decades after Roosevelt's death in 1945 and still gives hope to many ordinary Americans. By realigning government with ordinary workers and citizens, it created foundations for economic growth and a middle class who could make good on the American Dream. While the New Deal was not a revolutionary anti-capitalist regime and was far from an ideal democratic order, it resurrected the democratic dreams of the Declaration of Independence, reversed the corrupting legacy of two earlier corporate regimes, and demonstrates to skeptics today that U.S. regime change can take back the government from the corporate moguls.

ENTER, THE THIRD CORPORATE REGIME

The New Deal regime survived almost fifty years, profoundly changed the nation, helped enshrine the labor movement as a new force, and redefined the Democratic Party. But it, too, succumbed, as neoconservative radicals in the 1970s spurred a politics of regime change leading to the election of Ronald Reagan in 1980. In Chapter 3, I explore the many reasons for this all-important regime change, as dramatic as the one engineered by Rockefeller and Morgan. As a new generation of robber barons entered into a marriage with the Reaganite political class in Washington, they created a regime whose power is now compared with the Roman and British Empires. It rules not only America but much of the world.

The *third* corporate regime is the house we live in today. George W. Bush is just the current master of the mansion. The basic design of this regime was established by Reagan a quarter-century ago.

MEET THE PILLARS OF THE THIRD CORPORATE REGIME

Dominant Institution—The Transnational Corporation
Corporate plutocrats own this house.

Mode of Politics—Corpocracy
Wealthy residents run the house, although all tenants have a vote.

Social Contract—Social Insecurity
Tenants have no long-term lease.

Foreign Policy—Empire
The house rules the neighborhood.

Ideology—The Corporate Mystique
The house claims tenants are free and announces it is open for business.

THE TRANSNATIONAL CORPORATION

The foundation pillar of the regime is the transnational corporation, the biggest concentration of cold cash in human history. The companies dominating the regime—giants such as Wal-Mart, General Motors, General Electric, Exxon, Citigroup, Bank of America, Verizon Communications, Phillip Morris, and Microsoft—are wealthier than most countries. Citigroup has total assets of over a *trillion* dollars, to be precise *one trillion, one hundred eighty-seven million!*[7] Wal-Mart employed 1.3 *million* workers in 2003.[8] General Motors' annual sales in 2000 were larger than the gross domestic product (GDP) of Hong Kong, Denmark, Thailand, Norway, Poland, South Africa, and 158 other countries.[9] Of the 100 largest economies in the world in 2001, 51 were corporations, and only 49 were countries (based on a comparison of corporate sales and country GDPs). Big business has existed under every U.S. regime since the Civil War, but the third corporate regime is creating a world where companies are replacing countries as the superpowers. They make the corporations of earlier regimes look like pygmies.

Two hundred corporations sit at the heart of the regime, led by the Top Ten. These Top Ten alone have *assets worth about $4 trillion.* That is $4,000,000,000,000! But you'd have to add on GM, Ford, J. P. Morgan Chase, Microsoft, and scores of other behemoths to get the picture. Four trillion dollars is just a fraction of the wealth controlled by the two hundred intertwined giant companies that control the regime.

These firms' size reflects the rise of a truly transnational corporation, whose unique global character is uniquely

CORPORATE SUPERPOWERS

Here are the Top Ten U.S. Corporations in 2003, ranked by *Forbes* magazine according to a Super-Index of sales, profits, assets, and market.[10] I have listed only assets here.

THE TOP TEN	A$SETS
1. General Electric	574,274,000,000
2. Citigroup	1,097,190,000,000
3. ExxonMobil	152,644,000,000
4. AIG	547,295,000,000
5. Bank of America	660,458,000,000
6. Wal-Mart Stores	94,552,000,000
7. Fannie Mae	887,257,000,000
8. Verizon Communications	167,468,000,000
9. IBM	96,484,000,000
10. Altria Group	87,540,000,000

threatening for U.S. workers. We have long had global corporations, but never the transnational form of company that—at lightning speed and on a mass scale—can transfer abroad production of virtually every good and service. Not just the size but also the distinctive reliance on foreign labor and the approach to global profits differentiate transnational firms and the third corporate regime from previous incarnations. Today's corporation has turned "trade" into something quite new: a way to use U.S. capital to employ cheap foreign labor at the expense of American jobs. Trade becomes an internal transfer within the global corporation itself, maximizing profit by uniting U.S. capital and technology with foreign workers unprotected by labor laws or regulations. This inevitably produces the mass outsourcing of jobs that has now exploded into one of the great political issues of our time, and it serves notice that the core economic interests of the third corporate regime will increasingly diverge from the interests of American workers and citizens.

Two hundred corporations, eighty-two of which are American, dominate the global economy, producing 27.5 percent of the world's total economic activity. The regime serves the U.S. companies most directly but promotes global trade and investment rules benefiting all the top two hundred. Their combined sales are now greater than the combined economies of all countries minus the biggest ten, and eighteen times the combined annual income of the 1.2 billion people (24 percent of the total world population) living in "severe" poverty.

What do all these numbing numbers mean? For one thing, huge inequality. The top three shareholders of Microsoft own more money than do all six hundred million people in Africa. Bill Gates and Warren Buffet, the two richest corporate moguls, have more wealth than the poorest fifty million Americans. Beyond this, corporations make out like bandits in many ways. *The share of federal taxes paid by corporations dropped from 23.2 percent in 1960 to 11.4 percent in 1998.*[11] *In 1998, Texaco, Chevron, Pepsi Co., Enron, WorldCom, McKesson, and the world's biggest corporation, General Motors, paid no federal taxes at all.*[12]

In the third corporate regime, we are all corporate constructions. We get our dreams and opinions from corporate media such as Fox or Disney; our children's education is based on curricula provided by Microsoft or AT&T; our food comes from Phillip Morris and Wal-Mart, the world's largest grocers; our credit cards and mortgages are granted by one-stop superbanks such as Citigroup or J. P. Morgan Chase. Corporations pry away from government anything that is profitable and increasingly deliver our education, health care, social services, and even law enforcement. Everything is for sale since the regime's purpose is to promote profit above all else.[13]

As they seek to make the entire social order profitable and marketable, corporations are remaking everything in their own image, including government itself. Governments look and act more like companies, and corporations present themselves more as governments. Governments act to protect profits, and corporations speak the language of social responsibility. Business takes on the planning and rule-making roles of government, and government becomes increasingly about money.[14]

CORPOCRACY

OK, it's not a pretty word, but it describes an ugly reality. To understand corpocracy, look at George W. Bush's cabinet, a Who's Who of corporate America.[15]

PRESIDENT GEORGE W. BUSH
Former CEO of Texas Rangers and Board of Directors of Harken Energy

VICE PRESIDENT RICHARD CHENEY
Former CEO of Halliburton, Inc., the huge energy and defense conglomerate

SECRETARY OF DEFENSE DONALD RUMSFELD
Former CEO of General Instrument Company and
of the drug giant G. D. Searle and Co.

FIRST BUSH SECRETARY OF TREASURY PAUL O'NEILL
Former CEO of Alcoa and of International Paper Co.

SECRETARY OF THE TREASURY JOHN SNOW
Former CEO of CSX, the railroad giant, and
Chairman of the Business Roundtable, the leading
big business group in America

TRANSPORTATION SECRETARY NORMAN MINETTA
Former Corporate Vice President of Lockheed Martin

LABOR SECRETARY ELAINE CHAO
Former Vice President of Bank of America

AGRICULTURE SECRETARY ANN VENEMAN
Former Board of Directors of Calgene, Inc.,
a subsidiary of Monsanto Corporation

Bush's cabinet illustrates the marriage between big
business and big government that is the second pillar of today's corporate regime. Corporations are the senior partners in the marriage, dominating the political class because
of their control over election funding and the media and
the general triumph of big money over all major social
institutions. I call the marriage "corpocracy," since it represents corporate rule in a constitutional democracy and
turns a formally democratic government into a vehicle for
corporate ends. To be blunt: call it "pseudo-democracy."

Give due credit to Reagan for this second pillar. Despite
Reagan's rhetoric that "big government is the enemy," he
hugely expanded the vast, unaccountable federal government, a body so entangled with big business as to be indis-
tinguishable from it. Reagan's cabinet of former CEOs, like
Bush's, functioned as a Board of Directors for corporate

THE REGIME
AND MAD COW

After a "mad cow" was discovered in the United States, in December 2003, Alisa Harrison, the spokesperson for Agriculture Secretary Ann Veneman, told the American public **not to worry**—American beef is safe. She didn't say that she used to be public relations director of the National Cattlemen's Beef Association. In fact, the Department of Agriculture, which is supposed to protect the public from mad cow disease and other health risks, is packed with cattle and former ag-business lobbyists. Dale Moore, who is Veneman's chief of staff, was previously chief of staff for the National Cattlemen's Beef Association. And another high-ranking Department of Agriculture official used to be president of the National Pork Producers Council.[16]

America. True, Reagan dismantled much of the government created by the New Deal regime in the name of returning power to the people and the states. But he simply shifted government control and resources in a new direction. The system annually funnels billions of dollars in subsidies to corporations, whose financial power dominates the president's cabinet and congressional cloakrooms.

Corpocracy works like a Las Vegas slot machine, but one with a surefire chance of winning. Take the pharmaceutical industry as an example. In 2000, the industry put millions in the Washington slot machine to help reelect Bush.

THE CORPOCRACY GAME

RULES FOR DRUG COMPANIES

1. Give Bush $21 million during his 2000 campaign.
2. Spend $100 million in contributions, entertainment, and lobbying of Congress between elections (2000–2004).
3. Use 467 lobbyists on the Hill to pressure representatives and draft the Medicare Overhaul Bill, which returns billions in new profits to pharmaceutical companies.
4. Spend $100 million in 2004 to reelect the president and make sure that the new Medicare program delivers the goods.[17]

Of course, the game is not played just by pharmaceuticals. With all corporations pulling together, it's even more fun and profitable.

RULES FOR ALL CORPORATIONS

1. Give Bush $2 billion during his 2000 campaign.
2. Get back $300 billion in corporate welfare.
3. Draft the laws on energy, trade, media, pharmaceuticals, and health care.
4. Laugh all the way to the bank with a trillion-dollar tax bonanza.
5. Spend $3 billion in 2004 to reelect the president.

The industry then used its lobbyists in the House of Representatives to draft the huge Medicare overhaul bill passed in 2003. Yes, you're right, this bill prevents government bulk purchasing of pharmaceuticals, which might reduce prices and drug-company profits. And it will privatize Medicare, adding billions of dollars in profits to HMOs and private health insurers. And for good measure, the industry will give millions more in 2004 to help reelect the president and ensure the profits go where promised.

The New Deal remade government to serve and empower ordinary people, but today's regime is turning American democracy into a system of corporate sovereignty, creating a massive divide between rich and poor in political power as well as wealth. Corporations control the political agenda of both parties, and money washes away the people's voice. Citizens became consumers and couch potatoes, spectators of the show in Washington or indifferent to it. Workers like David Billingsly lose their voices and, increasingly, their jobs.

Just as troubling to a functioning democracy as classic quid pro quo corruption is that danger that officeholders will decide issues not on the merits or the desires of their constituencies, but according to the wishes of those who have made large financial contributions valued by the officeholder.

U.S. SUPREME COURT, *in a 2003 decision upholding campaign finance reform*

SOCIAL INSECURITY

The regime is systematically dismantling the social contract of the New Deal that promised social security to a generation traumatized by the Depression. That contract was expensive and protected people by regulating corporate excesses. The current regime seeks a new social contract—its third pillar—that trades the social security of workers and citizens for profit maximization.

Social insecurity begins with the job. The regime now aims to abolish the very concept of a job, the secure full-time form of work that prevailed in the mid twentieth century but now is seen as an unacceptable limit on profits. "What is disappearing," writes organizational analyst William Bridges, "is not just a certain number of jobs—or jobs in certain industries . . . but the very thing itself: the job. That much sought after, much maligned social entity, a job, is vanishing like a species that has outlived its evolutionary time."[18]

Jobs that survived in the new regime lost their government or union protections. This required all-out assault on the New Deal Wagner Act, which enshrined unions, and President Reagan was up to the task. The regime wasted no time in busting unions, with Reagan's first act being the dismantling of PATCO, the air traffic–controller union. Reagan then began what is now a long-standing regime policy of breaking unions: he made anti-union appointments to government labor boards, encouraged companies to break union contracts and demand concessions, and facilitated the ultimate corporate weapon against labor, exit power. As companies under the new regime fled overseas for cheap labor, aided by Reagan's tax breaks for companies operating overseas, massive downsizing became the regime's signature. Thus, the regime created the breed of contingent and outsourced jobs that has turned America's "middle class" into an "anxious class."

MEET ALLEN MARDSDEN

In my interviews I talked to many downsized and outsourced workers. Allen is a forty-year-old software engineer freelancing for computer companies in the United States and living in Boston. Allen told me that his father "was a salesman for an electrical company, and he worked for the same company his whole life." But Allen, although well educated with graduate degrees in business and accounting, has worked "for about forty companies," and, he says, "Fifty percent of the employees on the payroll are temp or contractors like me. The companies don't want to pay benefits, and they're greedy." Allen claims his father's era is finished, and Allen does not expect to ever get a permanent job.

By stripping away the protections and security of the New Deal job, the current regime is endangering the middle class. Allen declares flatly: "The middle class is disappearing." Like David, the despondent accountant profiled earlier, Allen says his own American Dream is shrinking. "Lots of things I thought I was going to have I may never have. I may never own a home. I may never marry, and I definitely will not have children." Allen is thinking not just of his own difficult economic circumstances but of his brother and sister-in-law, who have four children and are not making it. His brother has been downsized twice out of well-paying corporate jobs. Allen says, "My brother is on his second wife and was never in a position to afford even one."

In a transnational corporate regime, corporate globalization becomes the ultimate hammer for beating down U.S. job protections and security in the name of "free trade." But, as noted earlier, "trade" has become simply a vehicle by which U.S. transnational companies use American capital and technology to employ foreign rather than U.S. workers, outsourcing jobs and using the threat of future outsourcing to erode the benefits, protection, and security of the American worker created by the New Deal regime. The U.S. social contract is dragged down toward the horrendous social contract that has long prevailed in Third World countries, thereby globalizing the third corporate regime's social contract on terms that favor the transnational corporation at the expense of workers in both rich and poor countries.

Along with the loss of secure jobs and benefits, a horrendous social contract emerged from the slash-and-burn approach to the New Deal social welfare system. Reagan started the process by taking a sledgehammer to domestic social spending, arguing that the New Deal's welfare system undermined the entrepreneurial spirit at the heart of the new regime. He bled nearly every domestic program—education, health care, food stamps—to finance his huge tax cuts for the rich and his bloated military spending.

Reagan's social policies continued under Bush, Sr., and into the Clinton years, when Newt Gingrich spearheaded the Contract for America, which proposed cutting nearly all social spending and leaving a government devoted entirely to corporate welfare and the military. Clinton did his part by calling for "the end of welfare as we know it." Clinton targeted one hundred thirty federal programs for extinction, many for education, scientific research, or the environment, and he proposed to abolish or radically downsize the Department of Housing, the Department of Transportation, and other agencies devoted to social ends. One Washington observer noted, "You expect to see Republicans when they are in power doing this—it's what they've been pushing for years. But to see the Democrats doing it, and to see the competition between the White House and the Congress as they race to privatize—it's amazing."[19]

Bush is pursuing the regime's social contract in yet more brazen ways, openly promoting permanent tax cuts for the rich worth trillions of dollars while underfunding virtually all vital social programs, including his own touted education act, "Leave No Child Behind." In Chapter 7 I describe Bush's "war at home"—his assault on the social needs of ordinary Americans—which rivals the fierceness of his war on Iraq. Let it suffice to note here the regime's contract of Social Insecurity is moving, under Bush, toward its ultimate conclusion: privatizing and ultimately eliminating Social Security itself. The collapse and scandals of the financial markets postponed Bush's plans until his second term, but he proposed privatization in his 2004 State of the Union address, and his advisors are candid that they remain committed to privatizing Social Security and turning it from a scheme of social insurance into a private system of investments. That system not only threatens the retirement security of millions of lower- and middle-income Americans but also guarantees a multibillion-dollar bonanza for the Wall Street managers who are salivating about the profits to be made on your retirement money and mine.

EMPIRE

As it revolutionizes life at home, the corporate regime is bent on transforming the rest of the world, distinguishing itself from the corporate regimes of the Gilded Age and Roaring Twenties. The foreign policy aim of the current regime—its fourth pillar—is to shape a *global* corporate order under the political and military direction of the United States. That aim reflects the globalization of the economy, the increasing dependency of American corporations on profits abroad, the post–World War II collapse of the European empires, and intractable global crises that require military solutions. These elements combine to create a militarized corporate system, breeding a new form of empire and a system at home eroding classic American civil liberties.

Empire has a long American history, but the current regime is pulling out all the stops, dismantling much of the multilateral framework and the system of international law created under the New Deal. Remember that Roosevelt helped create the United Nations, and his regime successors, such as Truman and Eisenhower, pursued global power with some deference to multilateralism and U.N. conventions. Reagan was impatient with international treaties and other multilateral restraints on American power. He rejected the entire New Deal international framework, openly expressing contempt for the United Nation, arms control, and restraints on military spending. The new regime's corporate patrons encouraged Reagan's inclination to use American power unilaterally, including efforts to change regimes throughout Central America and elsewhere in the Third World, to open the world up to their own global greed.

President Bush has simply accelerated the regime tendencies begun under Reagan and pursued more quietly under Bush's father and Clinton. Maintaining Reagan's disdain for international law and his fondness for interventions and regime changes abroad, Bush has used the post-9/11 climate mainly to institutionalize these long-standing regime policies in an even more transparent model. Former White House advisor William A. Galston described the regime's current approach in its more extreme form: it "means the end of the system of international institutions, laws and norms that the U.S. has worked for more than half a century to build."[20] Princeton political scientist Richard Falk, one of the nation's leading scholars on international law, writes that the preemptive invasion of Iraq "repudiates the core idea of the United Nations charter. . . . It is a doctrine without limits, without accountability to the U.N. or international law."[21]

While the United States remains a constitutional system, the current U.S. regime already involves military expansion in the name of a war against evil, a fevered culture of patriotism and resurgence of religious nationalism, a system of growing repression and secrecy to protect "national security," the rise of a Homeland Security Department and a culture of surveillance, a weakening of traditional checks and balances, integration of corporations and the military, and the rise of a master ideology and political culture organized around "spin" and deception. These tendencies have been most developed by the Bush administration but are consistent with the regime's enduring aims of global dominance. They have raised serious alarms not just among liberals, but among many conservatives, from for-

HAVE YOU HAD THIS EXPERIENCE?

While driving in Boston recently, I saw a big, official-looking sign posted on the back of a city bus. It showed images of duct tape, flashlights, and water bottles, and it featured a face with a large eye looking right at me. The sign read, "Help everyone be safe by keeping your eye on the system." I felt a chill run down my back as I realized the sign was really saying, "Keep an eye on your neighbors," a Homeland Security directive right out of Orwell's *1984*.

mer Nixon advisor Pat Buchanan to the international financier George Soros, who see the specter of an Orwellian future. It is easy to see their point.

THE CORPORATE MYSTIQUE

Free markets! Free trade! Free people! Free Iraq! Free world! Free after-Thanksgiving sales! Freedom is the seductive mantra of the third corporate regime. Most Americans buy it.

Liberty, of course, has always been at the heart of American ideology. What is new is a rhetoric of freedom for all that translates into unimagined freedom for big business, and big problems for the rest of us. The expansion of freedom for the First Citizens of this regime (that is, the corporations) is now equated with personal freedom. When we increase the freedom of corporations to speech or privacy, we increase our own. If we limit corporate free speech by limiting corporate campaign contributions, we threaten the cherished First Amendment speech rights of citizens.

It is all part of the corporate mystique, the regime's ideology telling us that a "free market," based on unfettered corporate liberty, is the best of all possible worlds. The mystique says there really is no other way. The market's freedom is the cornerstone of every citizen's freedom, and a free corporation is the precondition to a free society. The corporation is the golden goose, but it needs free range. When freed to do what it wants, it delivers the goods. If we shackle it, we shackle ourselves and our prospects for the good life. Kill corporate freedom and we kill off democracy.

The mystique, while rhetorically embracing personal

liberty, in truth nourishes one form of personal freedom: the right to splurge at the mall. Consumerism! It is the highest form of freedom in the corporate mystique, and the regime encourages us to use our plastic cards to keep consuming long after we can afford to. Consumerism replaces citizenship as the operative value in the regime. *I buy, therefore I am. I am what I buy!*

The freedom dreamed of by the Founders is at high risk. Citizen choice in this regime is the right to decide between Coke and Pepsi. The regime argues that choice at the marketplace is the most powerful act of citizenship. One dollar, one vote. *That* is the democracy of the corporate mystique.

The regime then gets away with its frightening restraints on personal civil liberties, symbolized by the notorious Patriot Act. Citizenship is redefined as freedom in the mall, not the town hall. A corporate regime is seductive since we grew up as kids addicted to magical corporate goodies, whether Disney films or PCs. Creature comforts are the great blessings of the regime, and they are not easily dismissed by anyone, especially a population brought up on Toys 'R Us and wild about Big Macs. How can you challenge the producers of the Magic Kingdom, who have brought you happiness your whole life? How can you challenge the makers of Mickey Mouse, your best friend for life?

The corporate mystique, and its consumerist brand of democracy, was born in the first corporate regime and turned into a national religion in the second corporate regime of the Roaring Twenties. But in the earlier corporate regimes, leading ideologues were busy enough persuading the ordinary American to embrace the corporation

and get serious about consuming. Now they have to persuade the rest of the world. Globalization is the spread
of the corporate mystique as the universal religion of the
planet, and it is the cutting edge of the third corporate
regime's ideology.

One of the chief ideologues of globalization, *New York
Times* columnist Thomas Friedman, writes that "So ideologically speaking, there is no more mint chocolate chip,
there is no more strawberry swirl, and there is no more
lemon-lime. Today, there is only free-market vanilla."[22]
Nobody puts the regime's line better than Friedman. Corporations are not good and necessary for the happiness
only of Americans but of everyone in the world. And even
if you don't like it, you better learn to, because the train is
out of the station and can't be turned around. "I feel about
globalization a lot like I feel about the dawn. Generally
speaking, I feel it's a good thing that the sun comes up every
morning, . . . But even if I didn't much care for the dawn
there isn't much I could do about it. . . . I'm not going to
waste my time trying."[23]

This is the corporate mystique as God's way. The regime
aims to make everyone on the planet a believer.

THE SIX REGIME SINS

Six trends have hit the headlines under Bush that reveal
the long-term basic aims of the larger regime. If the pillars
of the regime create the design of the "house," these sins
are the design flaws that will lead to its inevitable destruction. We have here a mansion with a luxurious upper floor
and a deteriorating foundation. Even as the architects are
busily expanding the mansion, walls are crumbling, plumb-

ing is rusting, and the roof is leaking. All these things hint
that the regime, or political house, is beginning to implode
and decay.

1. Hooverism Redux

Bush is the only American president other than Herbert Hoover to preside over a net loss of jobs in the
economy, at this writing 2.6 million of them. The mass
loss of full-time unionized manufacturing jobs, along
with long-term wage stagnation and the relentless
stripping of overtime, pensions, health care, and
other benefits, has been a defining feature of the
regime for the past quarter-century. As it did under
Hoover, the regime trusts in business as it moves the
country and the world toward a speculative financial
capitalism, chronic macroeconomic instability, erratic
growth, and potential systemic deflation or depression. In this sense, Hooverism is the economic
Achilles heel of every corporate regime, expressing
itself now in global deregulation, overproduction,
and financial instability.

2. The Red Shift

One of the key signs of systemic erosion is the scary
red shift in the national accounts. Reagan led the way
when he cut taxes and increased military spending,
creating huge new debts. The Bush administration
has created the biggest budget deficits in American
history, amounting to $378 billion in fiscal year 2003
and projected to be almost half a trillion dollars the
following year. The current Bush deficits are bigger,

as a share of GDP, than those of Argentina when it melted down in 2002. Combined with massive trade deficits, the budget deficits put into serious question the fiscal credibility of a country depending on Japanese, German, Chinese, Saudi, and other foreign investment to finance its multitrillion-dollar national debt. The regime's priorities of high military spending, giant corporate subsidies, and enormous tax cuts ensure growing long-term debt. Bush pushes tax cuts, military spending, and deficits to the limits, thereby endangering the health of the economy and the regime he represents.[24]

3. Reverse Robin Hood

Every corporate regime is Robin Hood in reverse. The deficits from Reagan to Bush, Jr., grew out of manic tax cutting to achieve the corporate regime's main aim: transferring wealth to the rich. Trumping Reagan's, Bush's successive income tax cuts, projected to amount to several trillion dollars over the coming decade, are the most spectacular giveaway to the rich in American history. The top four hundred families, under Bush, gained the highest percentage of national income in more than half a century; the top 1 percent of the U.S. population control 40 percent of the wealth, their biggest slice of the American pie since the 1920s.[25] During the first twenty years of the regime, "the gap between rich and poor more than doubled from 1979 to 2000. . . . The gulf is such that the richest 1 percent of Americans in 2000 had more money to spend after taxes than the bottom

40 percent."[26] Between 1973 and 2000, average real income of the bottom 90 percent of Americans fell 7 percent. The top 1 percent saw their income rise 148 percent, the top .1 percent had a 343 percent income rise, and the top .01 percent had a 599 percent income rise.[27] America looks increasingly like Third World economies made up of corporate aristocrats and paupers.

4. Good-Bye, Social Welfare, Hello, Corporate Welfare

Bush has accelerated the regime's twenty-five-year trend toward brutally cutting social services—including education, Social Security, and health care—privatizing the shrunken remains, and redirecting federal savings to corporate welfare such as farming subsidies, mining and timber giveaways, research and development breaks and subsidies for big pharmaceuticals, depreciation breaks, and huge contracts to military companies. By the mid 1990s, according to the conservative Cato Institute, the regime was already spending approximately three hundred billion dollars a year on corporate welfare, reflecting the cronyism at the regime's heart.[28] The biggest service cuts and corporate welfare are still to come, laid out in the Bush administration's plans to privatize Social Security, Medicare, and the other programs at the heart of the New Deal. The Bush plan will turn over billions to the Wall Street houses that invest the new privatized retirement accounts, and to the health care companies that take over administration of Medicare, thereby undermining the retirement nest egg and key health care needs of most Americans as they age. But the war at home does not discriminate against the elderly; young people are the fastest growing group of poor in the twenty-five years of the regime, reflecting ever deeper cuts in education, child care, and welfare.[29]

5. Corporate Constitutionalism

Rewriting the Constitution to protect corporations rather than people has been a dominant theme of corporate regimes since the Gilded Age. Under the First, Fourth, Fifth, Sixth, Seventh, and Fourteenth Amendments, the Supreme Court has been extending constitutional protections to corporations, securing the corporate right to spend literally billions of dollars, through political action committees (PACs) and "soft money," on political campaigns and Washington lobbying, immune from public scrutiny. In the Reagan years, this was the perfect breeding ground for the savings and loan scandals and for huge corruption in the Pentagon and other government agencies. Today, the rash of Enron accounting scandals, Putnam mutual fund fraud, and Wall Street currency trading scandals reflect the same regime tendencies that weaken regulation and corporate accountability. Bush's new frontier involves coercively exporting legal protection for corporations to the rest of the planet under the auspices of the World Trade Organization

(WTO), which encompasses in its trade rules a planetary version of inviolable corporate rights in the name of free trade, development, and the war against terror.[30]

6. Global Imperialism

The United States has been expansionist since its beginning, but the third corporate regime has been the most imperialist and militarist on a planetary scale. Reagan massively built up the military and the military-industrial complex and engineered multiple regime changes abroad—most famously in Nicaragua, Grenada, and other Central American countries—in the name of anti-Communism. While his backers claimed that Reagan's policies created regime change in the Soviet Union itself, the Soviet Union, much like the Roman Empire, crumbled from within mainly because of its own corruption and inefficiency. After the Soviet meltdown, Bushes I and II both warred in Iraq to create a world order run solely by the United States. A long-standing regime aim is to integrate the petroleum reserves in the Middle East and elsewhere; the overarching goal is to increase the global profitability of American firms by preventing the rise of rival empires or trading blocs. Geopolitics and planetary greed meld in the new military-corporate regime, which now justifies its global imperialism in the name of a permanent war on terrorism.

CHAPTER 2

SNOOZING, TIPPING, AND WAKING UP

MEET MARK MELNER

Mark Melner is in his early forties, a hard worker who has been around the block a few times. He's a big, heavy fellow, well over two hundred pounds, and he has an eleventh-grade education. For most of the past fifteen years, Mark has been a security guard getting assignments from a private contracting firm, but he's had scores of different jobs over the years. He's seen presidents come and go, but he claims his life doesn't change from one election to the next.

Mark tells me that over most of the past twenty years, "I had three jobs going at the same time." He says, "I could survive with two jobs," but he's making about $5.50 or

$6.00 an hour, and he doesn't have health care benefits that he needs for his diabetes.

He's a part-timer now at Star Market, and "it's too much for part-time." He never knows what his hours will be, but they're often evening shifts that require he close the store at 11:30 p.m. He says, "I hate those hours [because] I don't have a car and the last bus you miss and you got to walk home." That can take a couple of hours when you're tired.

I ask Mark about the difference between full-time and part-time work. "Money and benefits. Everybody needs health care." He said he had really hoped that President Clinton would pass universal health care—"I definitely favored his health care program"—but Clinton was like the other presidents and didn't deliver.

Mark is worried now because his phone was just cut off. He can't get work without a phone since the contracting agency has to reach him early in the morning to tell him which job to go to that day. "I just have taken care of the electric bill and the unpaid several-month phone bill is at least $150. Everything else is pretty well caught up and I just paid my rent." The $150 for the phone would clean him out.

Mark's been wanting to marry Marina for a long time. But he says both he and Marina would need full-time jobs to pay for the wedding, and they haven't found them yet.

People like Mark say they don't vote because they don't think the result will change their lives. You can call Mark an irresponsible couch potato, but he has a point. Mark has seen very little change in his life over the past twenty years, whether a Republican or Democratic president is in the White House. Only certain kinds of elections are likely to make a difference for people like Mark—these are the un-usual ones that lead to regime change.

There is no necessary relation between regime change and elections, and I have yet to explain how they do con-nect. In this chapter and the next one, I take a look back at earlier elections. I'll bet you want to jump ahead to 2004 and beyond, but the history is vitally important. What you learn from history is that elections usually do not cre-ate regime change. To understand 2004 and 2008, and to figure out how to get workers such as Mark interested, means looking back to discover why most elections have left them cold.

Historically, we have had three types of American elec-tions. The first are *regime-changing* elections that usher in a new order. The second are *status quo* elections that perpetuate the existing regime and create no movement toward regime change, even if the party controlling the White House changes. The third are *regime-tipping* elec-tions that dramatically weaken or radicalize the regime but

POP QUIZ

HOW DO YOU CLASSIFY THE 2004 ELECTIONS? PICK ONE:

- ☐ Regime-Changing
- ☐ Status Quo
- ☐ Regime-Tipping

do not create decisive regime change. They open up new vistas but do not cause the regime to fall in the short term. The only kind of elections likely to pique the interest of Mark, David, and other workers are those that are regime-changing or regime-tipping; the rest will be less interesting to most ordinary Americans than the sitcom on prime time.

REGIME CHANGE WITH BALLOTS

We had only a small number of regime-changing elections in the past century. The two main ones were the 1932 election of Franklin D. Roosevelt and the 1980 election of Ronald Reagan, both worth telling your grandkids about.

THE GREATEST ELECTION

Roosevelt's election in 1932 ended the Roaring Twenties' corporate regime and ushered in the New Deal regime, which reshaped the balance of power and the American way of life for almost half a century. The hope was so palpable it seemed as though millions of Americans were singing "Happy Days Are Here Again." During FDR's inaugural address in 1933, he proclaimed, "The only thing we have to fear is fear itself," after which a New Deal historian wrote that Roosevelt's words "made his greatest single contribution to the politics of the 1930s: the instillation of hope and courage in the people."[1] But right after making his famous statement about fear, Roosevelt attacked the nation's elite bankers in the same inaugural: "We are stricken by no plague of locusts. . . . Plenty is at our doorstep." Then the president, breathing fire, went where most presidents are afraid to go:

Rulers of the exchange of mankind's goods have failed through their own stubbornness and their own incompetence. ... The money changers have fled from their high seats in the temple of civilization. We may now restore that temple to the ancient truth.[2]

Strong words! This was the sign that regime change was coming, followed by the famous "hundred days" that sacked Hoover's corporate regime and replaced it with the most activist regime of government planning and social protection in American history.

Several events converged to make this possible, the most important being the Great Depression. The collapse of the economy led Americans to raise questions about capitalism that are rarely entertained in the United States, and to force these questions into the electoral process. Take note: When the economy goes seriously awry, Americans will take down the regime with ballots.

We're not talking revolution here. The New Deal did more to preserve capitalism than to undermine it. Charles Edison, the president of Thomas A. Edison, Inc., was so impressed with Roosevelt's initial fiscal conservatism and consultation with business that he put plaques on his factory walls for the public to see, "President Roosevelt has done his part, now you do something. Buy something ... paint your kitchen, send a telegram, give a party ... This old world is starting to move again."[3]

But while Roosevelt kept faith with some business sectors, the New Deal brought real regime change that led many big business leaders to denounce Roosevelt as a "class traitor." It *reinterpreted the Constitution* by shifting fundamental rights to ordinary citizens rather than big business; in the famous 1934 Blaisdell case, the U.S. Supreme Court ruled in favor of a Minnesota law that allowed hard-pressed tenants to breach their contracts with landlords and banks, a decision that altered the sanctity of corporate contracts in the name of social justice for years thereafter. Roosevelt created what New York Senator Robert Wagner called the beginning of "a nationally planned economy"—*Communist-sounding* words nobody expressed or really even fantasized about in the America of Coolidge and Hoover. That's what regime change does—it takes what is treason in the last regime and makes it the law of the land! With the 1935 Wagner Act and Social Security Act, the New Deal helped create the modern labor movement and a new welfare state, everything the Roaring Twenties regime viewed as betraying the Constitution. These were the key changes in the past hundred years that helped make the hardscrabble lives of people like Mark better. The New Deal reenergized grassroots politics and juiced up the social movements that got couch potatoes off their couches.

THE GREATEST CORPORATE ELECTION

The 1980 election was another regime-changing one, since the Reagan Revolution put a decisive end to the New Deal regime and made progressives like me pull out their already thinning hair. Like Roosevelt, Reagan brought a new spirit to America, saying in his inaugural, "What I want to see above all else is that this remains a country where someone can always get rich." To create what he called his "revolution for entrepreneurs," he dismantled most of the protections that the New Deal had created for workers such as Mark. After Reagan's inaugural on January 20, 1981, I'd wager executives uncorked more Champagne bottles in the boardrooms of America than they did at home on New Year's Eve.

Reagan's regime change did not arise from a calamity like the Depression, but it did emerge from serious economic crises. Remember the 1970s, with spiking gas prices, prolonged stagflation, and interest rates over 20 percent? If you don't, ask Jimmy Carter, who went down with the old regime as the economy tanked.

Competition from Japan and Europe dramatically changed U.S. corporate strategy in the 1970s and helped Reagan bring down the regime. To survive global competition and—even better—to escape and undermine New Deal regulation and unions, U.S. corporations got smart. Their new strategy was bold: move operations abroad to Mexico, Indonesia, and the ripest plum, China. Target American manufacturing, the unionized sector where the New Deal had most powerfully entrenched itself. Exploit Reagan's aggressive "free trade" policies, including those that gave tax breaks to corporations moving offshore. Use exit power—the ability to leave the United States and set up plants abroad—to break the back of American labor and undermine the main political force behind the New Deal.

This Great Corporate Awakening radically shifted the overall domestic balance of power. Since the 1935 Wagner Act, labor's strength had been the key to the survival of the New Deal regime. The globalization of capital markets and the strategy of corporate flight was the last gasp for the New Deal regime. For workers and many middle-class folks, it's no secret that Reagan changed the regime.[4]

Reagan's regime change unhinged the great American middle class that the New Deal created, making it perpetually insecure. Consider Earnest, a thirty-five-year-old telecommunications worker whose company began a series of major downsizings soon after Reagan's election in the 1980s. Earnest grew up in the "old" New Deal regime, was accustomed to permanent well-paying work, and saw what happens when others like him got hit in the face with the realities of an election breeding real regime change. He tells a graphic story of workers' anxieties as they faced chronic downsizing and the demise of the old regime. His company, which had never—before Reagan—downsized a single worker in its seventy-five years, changed course in the 1980s and

let go of all the in-house temporaries, first. Then they combined departments. Then they started chopping departments off, and combining the jobs of the departments, while increasing the job descriptions of the people who were doing the jobs. Then they're cutting back on benefits. They had this thing where they had a meal voucher. Every time you worked two hours overtime you would receive a nine-dollar meal voucher for the meal you missed. Then they took that away from people, and here people are working overtime that very day and counting on that for meals. And, I mean, the panic and the fear was just so thick you could cut it with a knife.

Earnest kept a positive attitude but fear spread fast.

I'd come in in the morning and I'd see people, and they were just stressed out. They didn't know how long they would have their job. The fear, it was like a snowball thing, beginning to roll downhill. The fear, the rumor mill, were rolling together, and they picked up speed. By the time they hit the employees, it was just overwhelming to them. People became sick from the panic. A couple of people died from heart attacks. One lady died in the parking lot. She only had five years on the job, so she was fearful she would be cut.

With downsizing a chronic fact of life, it is hardly stretching matters to describe it as a form of domestic terrorism, bred systemically shortly after Reagan's election. That is the way Earnest saw it—terror suddenly breaking out and spreading like a cancer through his company. But such terrorism could not have happened had the New Deal and its labor protections survived intact. Reagan's election in 1980 unleashed the regime change that created this systemic anxiety, molding the kind of "permanently temporary" or "temporarily permanent" work that now plagues almost the entire American workforce.

SNOOZE ELECTIONS

Most American elections are far less momentous than those of 1932 or 1980. They are status quo elections that basically sustain the existing order. Most Americans sleep right through them.

The most typical snooze, or status quo, elections are those that give a second term to the incumbent or turn the White House over to another president from the same party. Typical examples are the elections of Presidents Coolidge and Hoover, who both perpetuated the 1920s

GOP big business regime that started under Harding. The same was true of most of the elections in the Gilded Age, from 1872 to the end of the nineteenth century, when the presidency was handed from one Republican to another. Grover Cleveland was the lone Democrat elected during the whole period, in 1884 and again in 1892. While his two elections represented a shift in the party controlling the White House, they did not change the corporate regime. Cleveland, a business-friendly Democrat who was a forerunner of Bill Clinton and the DLC, sent a message right after the 1892 election: "No harm will come to any business interest through any administrative policy so long as I am president."[5]

He was true to his promise. Cleveland was honest and a modest reformer but did nothing to change or end the corporate regime of the robber barons. When labor leaders pleaded with him to send in troops to protect strikers during the famous 1894 Pullman strike, the beginning of a national strike, which took place in Pullman, Illinois, a tiny town just south of Chicago, Cleveland responded, "You might as well ask me to dissolve the government of the United States."[6]

A Gilded Age business leader wrote, *"It matters not one iota what political party is in power or what president holds the reins of office."*[7] He was right, sadly—now fast-forward one hundred years.

The year 1992 saw another election that changed the party but not the regime. Clinton had a different political philosophy than did Reagan and Bush, Sr., but he did not see himself as a New Dealer or a president who would challenge the corporate order. Clinton was the candidate of the rising DLC, which was recrafting the mainstream Democratic Party's vision and platform to accommodate the new corporate regime realities. Among Clinton's greatest hits:

Ending "welfare as we know it"
New "free-trade agreements," like NAFTA
More corporate welfare—$300 billion a year
Fiscal austerity—e.g., Rubin policy of zero deficits
Proposal to abolish/privatize one hundred thirty
    government agencies
Mantra of "small government"

Sound familiar? It should. Clinton actually pushed through many of the aims of the corporate regime that Reagan and Bush, Sr., had not completed.

Clinton was not a Reagan clone by any means. From environmental policies to foreign policy to social issues involving abortion, gun control, women's rights, and gay rights, Clinton had a different agenda. If Clinton had not been elected, the regime might have taken a far more conservative and dangerous turn under a second Bush, Sr., term. Thus even status quo elections can make a difference. But because 1992 and 1996 helped integrate the Democratic Party into the existing corporate regime, they were anything but regime-changing elections and actually made future regime change more difficult.

TIPPING BUT NOT TOPPLING

The third kind of election is what I call regime-tipping, which significantly weakens or otherwise alters a regime but does not topple it. These elections typically shift control of the White House from one party to another and create conditions for a future regime change. These are not elections like 1932 or 1980, which create decisive regime change, but don't ignore them! They plant the seeds for a new destiny.

THE 1968 ELECTION

In 1968 Lyndon Johnson did not run for a second term because of Vietnam. The replacement candidate, LBJ's vice president, Hubert Humphrey, was defeated, and Richard Nixon was elected. This was the beginning of the end of the New Deal, and 1968 was a tipping point.

But many conditions were not yet in place to allow Nixon to engineer regime change. The corporate shift toward a global strategy was in its earliest stage, and unions were still powerful enough to prevent wholesale erosion of the New Deal. In 1968, the civil rights movement and the anti–Vietnam War movement were creating a political culture to push the New Deal and the Democratic Party further to the left. Moreover, the neoconservatives and Christian fundamentalist activists who would help remake the Republican Party in the image of Senator Barry Goldwater and create the New Right movement were still in junior high school.

Nonetheless, the 1968 elections made an important difference. Humphrey might have ended the Vietnam War sooner, despite his support for it. He also would have tried to restart the Great Society, which might have saved the New Deal regime with fresh ideas. And while he distanced himself from the antiwar movement, he was aligned with the civil rights movement and wanted to aid that struggle and strengthen the New Deal's commitment to minorities and the dispossessed.

Nixon was a conservative, but he remained bound by the framework of the old regime, tipping it but not ending it. The fading New Deal regime still bound a right-winger like Nixon to its basic philosophy. *In fact, Nixon was to the left, on many domestic issues, of a Democratic corporate regime president like Clinton.* Consider now what Nixon, who got elected, actually did:

> Proposed a minimum income for all Americans
> Signed the law creating the Environmental Protection Agency (EPA)
> Signed the bill creating the Occupational Safety and Health Administration (OSHA)
> Created the Consumer Safety Product Commission

But Nixon's commitment to the Vietnam War, and his inflated military spending, helped erode the surplus that would have made it possible to sustain or increase New Deal social spending. He promoted globalization linked to militarism that accelerated under Reagan and became central to the new corporate regime. He mobilized a revolt of the "moral majority" against the civil rights and antiwar movement that might have sustained and deepened the New Deal. Moreover, his "moral majority" helped construct the base for the neoconservatives and New Right that transformed the Republican Party and created regime change in 1980. Nixon was a classic "tipper," destabilizing a regime he couldn't seem to escape.

Now we're getting to what most of you are waiting for! How do you classify the 2004 elections? Check what you picked in the Pop Quiz at the beginning of this chapter, and see if you still agree.

My answer: 2004 could be an important regime-tipping election, no matter who wins. It will not decisively create regime change. But it might tip the current regime dramatically, either by taking it far to the right if Bush wins or by undermining it if Democrats win and pursue regime change rather than normal politics. The stakes could not be higher!

Bush is the most extreme president of recent memory, and he is rapidly moving the current regime beyond its existing parameters. Control of both houses of Congress and the courts, as well as the White House, would dramatically increase the prospects of a right-wing regime turn toward an "antiterrorism" police state regime, further weakening constitutional democracy and promoting unaccountable corporate rule at home and abroad. Ironically, then, 2004 is regime-tipping. Bush himself, while he is likely to perpetuate the third corporate regime, could tilt it in an even more extremist direction and create a right-wing regime change in his second term.

If Bush loses, the current regime could be radically weakened in the opposite direction, laying the foundation for progressive regime change in future elections—*but it all depends on what the Democrats do.* Although the Democratic base is hopping mad, the Democratic Party establishment is still wedded to the current corporate regime. Despite some populist rhetoric among the 2004 candidates, party leaders are timid and thinking within this regime's box; they can hardly imagine what a real regime change would look like. It is thus very possible that a Democratic victory would simply preserve the current corporate regime, keeping it from tipping further right but not creating progressive regime change. Such change is inevitable in the long term because of the terminal regime crises I describe in later chapters, but it might not take place now. *Remember, Bush Lite still happens!*

A Democratic administration might, though, create a more favorable environment for the social movements that can transform the country, as I describe in Chapter 9. In the 1960s this happened under John F. Kennedy, a centrist Democrat who opened up more space for the rise of the civil rights and student movements than existed under Eisenhower. Eventually, emerging movements will mobilize millions of people like David, Mark, and Earnest, who sound like the workers Roosevelt rallied in 1932, one of whom said, "We are like the drounding man, grabbing at everything that floats by, trying to save what little we have."[8]

CHAPTER 3

NORMAL POLITICS ... NOT!

*T*homas Kuhn, the famed philosopher of science who wrote *The Structure of Scientific Revolutions,* showed that science develops through surprising transformations.[1] Kuhn says that science moves in dramatic leaps from one basic paradigm to another, rather than following an evolutionary process. These quantum leaps in science are something like regime changes in politics: they are disruptive and radical.

Kuhn says there are two ways to do science. In most periods, scientists play by the rules of *normal science.* They accept the reigning theoretical paradigm and try to solve the small puzzles yet to be resolved. But over time, inexplicable contradictions—Kuhn calls them "anomalies" —begin to accumulate. A few brave scientists question whether the reigning paradigm can explain the contradictions, and they embark on a heretical quest to topple it and construct a new paradigm. In the process, they move *beyond normal science*, a shift from defending and patching up the old order to creating a new one. A Newton or an Einstein eventually emerges and proposes a revolutionary theory. A growing number of radical scientists embrace it and work to establish it as a new order.[2]

Politics is no science—hey, everyone but political scientists knows that! But like normal science, there is the game of *normal politics*: Republicans played it through most of the New Deal and Democrats have been playing it ever since FDR died. When you play the game of normal politics, you treat the big questions as settled, making most political contests about small matters that do not shake the regime and do not change the lives of ordinary Americans.

The second political game is *regime change*, which the Democrats played during the creation of the New Deal and the Reagan Republicans played during the creation of today's regime. It is like science in its thrilling, quantum-leap phases. During the 1930s the Democrats were paradigm breakers, and in the 1970s and 1980s the Republicans were the quantum leapers. New Dealers during the Depression and New Righters at the opening of the Reagan Revolution made politics a far more visionary and exciting game than in normal eras. Even couch potatoes got inspired—they may have listened to FDR's fireside chats on their couch, but they were really paying attention and promising to work with the president to change the country.

Contradictions in today's regime have begun to reach a critical mass. The disastrous work experiences of millions of people, such as our despairing accountant, David Billingsly, are the kind of "anomaly" that is now near critical mass and will eventually blow the regime apart. But the Democrats keep playing the game of normal politics, which explains why workers like David and Mark (introduced in Chapter 2) have not been out working for the party.

NAME THEIR GAME

To start, take a little quiz on which leaders are regime changers and which play normal politics.

- ☐ George Bush, Sr.
- ☐ George W. Bush
- ☐ Wesley Clark
- ☐ Bill Clinton
- ☐ Howard Dean
- ☐ Dick Gephardt
- ☐ Al Gore
- ☐ John Kerry
- ☐ Dennis Kucinich
- ☐ Ralph Nader
- ☐ Ronald Reagan
- ☐ Franklin Roosevelt

See the answers at the end of this chapter. Expect some surprises!

As we approach 2004 and beyond, let us be clear about *the rules of regime change politics* that the Democrats (with a few exceptions, such as the late Senator Paul Wellstone) have forgotten and must now embrace. The New Dealers and the New Righters, the masters of the regime change game in the twentieth century, provide an abundance of examples of why this is so.

RULE 1: EMBRACE DEFEAT

It's hard enough to accept defeat, let alone to enthusiastically embrace it. But this is precisely what the New Righters did in 1964, when President Johnson crushed Arizona Republican Senator Barry Goldwater in a landslide. Goldwater had rejected the normal politics of Eisenhower Republicans in the 1950s and campaigned on a radical platform to overthrow the New Deal regime (well, he didn't quite put it that way, but that's what he wanted to do). It was a premature strategy, and Johnson flattened Goldwater like a pancake in one of the biggest Democratic victories of all time. The genius of the New Right was to reject conventional wisdom about Goldwater's humiliating defeat, refusing to skulk back to normal politics. *Instead, they embraced this big loser as a hero and saw in his candidacy the route to regime change in the decade to come. Democrats, take note!*

The Goldwater loyalists, sensing the vulnerabilities of the New Deal regime, saw that Goldwater had aroused a constituency in the Bible Belt that could revolutionize the country. Though Goldwater suffered a catastrophic national defeat, he had won the South and thereby created a situation ripe for a major political realignment (a sea change central to regime change today, as I show in Chapter 11). The New Deal regime had been based on a coalition between the historically rock-solid Democratic South and the industrial labor base in the Midwest. By winning the South, Goldwater shattered the political foundation of the New Deal and opened the path to the emergent coalition between Wall Street, Southwest military and energy corporations, and Southern religious fundamentalists that would become the base of the Reagan-Bush regime.[3]

The New Righters did not accept the rule of normal politics to shun the radical candidate and his ideas. Had they done so, they would have moved the Republican Party back to the center and put forward an Eisenhower candidate. Instead, embracing Goldwater in defeat, they shifted to regime change politics and built the insurgent party that led to the Reagan Revolution and today's regime. In the process, they created a historic political realignment that we desperately need again today.

When Al Gore lost in 2000, he took the opposite path from Goldwater, playing normal politics when he should have been promoting regime change. In the 1990s, Ross Perot famously described the "giant sucking sound" that was pulling manufacturing jobs out of the country and devastating the Democratic base; in so doing, Perot sounded a tentative call for regime change. But Gore supported the North American Free Trade Agreement (NAFTA) in a highly visible debate against Perot, clearly endorsing the globalization agenda central to the corporate regime. He trounced Perot in the debate but alienated many Democrats and Independents whose jobs were flying offshore. Gore, like Clinton, was a DLC Democrat whose whole career was the product of normal politics (until more recently, when he shocked the political world and endorsed insurgent Democratic candidate Howard Dean). His centrist presidential campaign is the rule in normal politics and came naturally to him, but it lost him the election.

Gore's defeat as an incumbent during relative peace and prosperity was as shattering as Goldwater's. Gore may have woken up in his Dean endorsement and finally embraced defeat, but the Democratic establishment has not. The Democrats will have to build an insurgent coalition of its working family base and the nonvoters and dissident social movements Gore lost through normal politics. These

GORE'S DREAM

It's easy to imagine that Gore is haunted by recurring thoughts while he dreams:

"If only I had opposed NAFTA or supported big changes in the structure of the treaty. If only I had been bolder and challenged my own party establishment, really spoken up for the people. I would have mobilized a far greater turnout of my Democratic base, especially the blue-collar workers bleeding from the trade and tax policies of the regime. I might have gotten the now famous 'race car' or NASCAR dads, mostly working-class, like the 'Reagan Democrats' who voted Republican. I might have gotten the majority of poor and working-class families who didn't come out and vote at all. I might have won the support of the rising antiglobalization movement and other populist forces rallying against big money in Washington who turned to Ralph Nader. I might have won. . . . I might have won."

Gore wakes up in a feverish sweat.

groups will continue to vote Republican, vote for third parties, or remain couch potatoes until the Democrats become regime changers.

RULE 2: PLAY OFFENSE, THINK BIG

In normal politics, the rule is to think small and play defense. It's an understandable strategy on the Boston highways and in many marriages, and it's the standard approach during most political eras. Since the regime is well established and parties seek to contest the White House without changing regimes, politics is about small ideas. With big ideas out of play, parties play defense by moving to the center, and politics loses its intellectual appeal; it becomes entertainment, about personalities and partisan horse races. Paradoxically, thinking small and playing defense have been embraced by the Democratic Party today, while the Bush Republicans are doing the opposite, thinking big and playing offense as they seek to push the envelope of the current corporate regime.

BIG-THINKING REPUBLICANS, SMALL-THINKING DEMOCRATS

In a dramatic, historic reversal of roles, the party that should be challenging the regime is playing normal politics, and those running the regime are exploiting a cardinal rule of regime change. The Bush Republicans are still following Goldwater, most famously remembered for his phrase "Extremism in the pursuit of liberty is no vice." The 1970s brash neoconservatives, still in power today and still pushing big ideas, happily embraced extremism from the beginning, forming foundations and journals and filling them with radical ideas. They have now accomplished some of their big (and mostly very bad) ideas:

Privatize Medicare
Privatize Social Security
Deregulate the mass media
Provide vouchers for private schools
Encourage home schooling
Abolish the estate tax
Institute the flat tax
Abolish taxes on corporate dividends
Eliminate most environmental regulations
Eliminate unions
Abolish the United Nations
Abolish the federal government (except the Pentagon
    and corporate welfare)

There was nothing modest or centrist in the thinking of these neoconservatives, or of the Reagan administration itself, whose explicit intent was to dismantle the New Deal once and for all while destroying the Soviet "Evil Empire." And today, these same neoconservatives, now the leading lights of the Bush administration, are still not playing normal politics, and they are still winning by refusing to move to the center and think small.

BIG-THINKING DEMOCRATS, SMALL-THINKING REPUBLICANS

The New Dealers were also thinking big in 1932. Franklin D. Roosevelt knew it was no time for normal politics or for appeasing the corporate establishment. In the Roaring Twenties, big ideas about laissez-faire, corporate self-regulation, and corporate paternalism had become deeply entrenched in the mainstream. After a period of vacillation and uncertainty, Roosevelt attacked all these ideas, willing to risk the label of class warfare that intimidates Democrats in eras of normal politics. Roosevelt became the first president to launch a European-style social democracy in America, and his raft of ideas saved capitalism—but only by radically changing the political conversation. His regime-changing ideas—normal politics in Europe but almost revolutionary in the United States—inspired the most important legislation of the twentieth century:

Social Security Act (created Social Security)
Wagner Act (legalized unions and collective bargaining)
Public Works Administration: Emergency Relief
    Appropriations Act (created big government
    programs to employ jobless workers)
Glass Steagall Act (strictly regulated banking and
    Wall Street)
Holding Company Act (broke up utilities and other
    big holding companies)
Rural Electrification Act (created public utilities)

Some of these ideas may seem like no big deal, but after the Hooverist "hands off" philosophy of the Roaring Twenties regime, they were mind-bending. The rich attacked it as socialism, but workers all over America found that politics finally meant something: a job, a voice, a little respect. These laws *created* the American middle class. No wonder so many people cried openly when they heard of FDR's death. Roosevelt turned the government from a handmaiden of the corporation into a countervailing power of and by the people, prepared to challenge business on key issues, including constitutional ones. Roosevelt's willingness to "pack the court" to shift the constitutionalism of the Gilded Age and the Roaring Twenties makes clear that he had rejected the politics of defense and small ideas.

Throughout FDR's four terms, the Democratic Party played offense, seeking to reverse the legacy of two prior corporate regimes. *The New Deal was the only time that the Democratic Party has ever embraced militant regime change politics, and it produced the only sustained period of Democratic ascendancy in American history. Shouldn't the Democratic Party leaders today be forced to repeat this lesson ten times at breakfast, ten times at lunch, ten times at dinner, and a hundred times before going to bed?*

WHEN THE DEMOCRATS STOPPED THINKING BIG

The New Deal declined partly because Roosevelt's successors did not continue the spirit of thinking big that Roosevelt himself pioneered. Despite having congressional majorities in the 1950s, 1960s, and 1970s, Democrats did not pursue the ambitious social goals that FDR himself might have embraced. The Democrats didn't try to build or democratize the labor movement. They didn't pass universal health care and they didn't attack corporate power. They bought into the Cold War and, in the 1960s, turned against the Left as it was pushing for participatory democracy at home and for peace, justice, and human rights in foreign policy—precisely what the Democratic Party should have been doing.

Thinking big and going on the offensive is necessary to create regime change and to sustain the regime over the long term. Admittedly, it is easier for Republicans to get major funding for their visionary ideas and politics, and Democratic visionaries have to run their institutes, magazines, and organizations on a shoestring. Democrats get corporate funding when they play the regime's game and take on the role of incremental reformers or the "loyal opposition." This explains the seduction of thinking small for the Democratic establishment, but it doesn't make it a good idea—in fact, it's criminal that the Democrats have prostituted themselves to their own corporate patrons. If it wants to win elections, the Democratic Party has to find other ways to spread the messages it needs to convey. Fortunately, the rise of the Internet as an inexpensive way to reach millions of people with bold ideas, and to raise small contributions, as Howard Dean did, from large numbers of "little people," suggest there are new ways for Democrats to think big and play offense.

Franklin Roosevelt introduced notions of social democracy into American politics, but his successors dropped the ball.[4]

TED NACE, *author of* Gangs of America

Ironically, in the past quarter-century, the Democratic Party has remained in the defense mode with its accompanying small ideas of normal politics, at the very historic moment when conditions are emerging for fresh ideas and regime change. As just noted, the neoconservatives remain the big thinkers and offensive players now dominating Washington, a remarkable phenomenon for a regime well into middle age and beginning to suffer the slings and arrows of regime reversals of fortune.

DEMOCRATS AS ADDICTS

The Democrats' addiction to normal politics is a bit like Nero fiddling while Rome burns.

RULE 3: MAKE YOUR PARTY A SOCIAL MOVEMENT

Most of us like parties, but we tend to stay home when it comes to the political parties these days. How many party caucuses or conventions have you been to? In normal politics, parties are establishments of professional politicians, not a home for ordinary citizens. Politics becomes a spectator sport for all but the political class. Citizens keep their distance from the parties because the latter are stifling bureaucracies with nothing to offer ordinary people.

REVOLT OF THE BIBLE BELT: NEW RIGHT POLITICS AS SOCIAL ACTIVISM

In regime change politics, new grassroots groups force themselves onto the political scene and penetrate the bureaucracy of the parties. The second phrase of Goldwater's famous declaration about extremism was "Moderation in the pursuit of justice is no virtue." This sounds more like a social movement credo than a political party platform. The New Right of the 1970s was very much a social movement of fire-and-brimstone Bible Belt preachers tied to an in-

surgent class of grassroots Southern conservative gun owners, religious fundamentalists, inspired New Right policy
wonks, and political organizers, such as direct mail expert
Richard Viguerie and Paul Weyrich, a founder of the Moral
Majority. In addition, a major movement of Fortune 500
and Wall Street corporate elites, who organized themselves to help dig the final grave of the New Deal and to
create a corporate regime, led and financed this regime
change politics.

The Goldwater campaign was the cauldron in which the
new conservative activists learned how to shake and rattle
the old regime. Here's how one New Righter described the
campaign:

> It was learning how to act: how letters got written, how
> doors got knocked on, how coworkers could be won
> over on the coffee break, how to print a bumper sticker,
> and how to pry one off with a razor blade. . . . how
> to talk to a reporter, how to picket, and how, if need
> be, to infiltrate—how to make the anger boiling inside
> you ennobling, productive, powerful, instead of embit-
> tering.[5]

Doesn't this sound like social activism to you? It was exactly what I was learning as a civil rights activist in Missis-
sippi at about the same time.

Christian grassroots groups eventually began to cross
paths with and cross-fertilize the thinking of more established regime change conservatives inside the Nixon and
Ford administrations, including Donald Rumsfeld, Paul
Wolfowitz, and Dick Cheney, as well as the corporate elites
on Wall Street. The Christian preachers fired up a Republican populist base in the churches of the South; the polit-

ical organizers linked them in a nationally coordinated and corporate-funded movement for change in Washington; and the policy wonks and intellectuals created the over-arching neoconservative vision to guide the movement and link it securely to the interests of the corporate and military establishment.[6]

THE SOCIAL MOVEMENT OF THE BOSSES

The New Right social activists would have been a footnote in history without the regime change campaign from the boardrooms. By the early 1970s, business had concluded that its relative weakness since the Roosevelt era meant that it was finally time to counterattack to end the New Deal. Influential corporate attorney Lewis Powell, later appointed to be a Supreme Court justice by Richard Nixon, wrote a memo to the Chamber of Commerce in 1971 stating, "As every business executive knows, few ele-ments of American society today have as little influence in government as American business, the corporation. . . . the business executive is truly 'the forgotten man.'" At 1974 and 1975 meetings of corporate leaders sponsored by the New York Conference Board, one participant continued this theme: "At this rate, business can soon expect support from the environmentalists. We can get them to put the corporation on the endangered species list."[7]

A full-scale corporate campaign began in the early 1970s, brilliantly chronicled by corporate historian Ted Nace, who dubbed it "The Revolt of the Bosses." It proves the critical point that social movements for regime change can arise among elites as well as among the grass roots. "Corporations of the World, Unite!" shows some of the

CORPORATIONS OF THE WORLD, UNITE!

1972   CEO Frederick Borch of General Electric and CEO
        John Harper of Alcoa formed the Business Round-
        table, an organization made up exclusively of CEOs
        from the biggest corporations of America.[8] The Busi-
        ness Roundtable became a forum for corporate co-
        ordination at the highest levels, lobbying for anti-
        union policies and procorporate tax, regulatory, and
        macroeconomic policies.

1972   Joseph Coors, the wealthy activist brewer, helped to
        found right-wing watering holes like the Heritage
        Foundation (originally the Analysis and Research As-
        sociation). Along with the American Enterprise In-
        stitute, the Heritage Foundation is one of the most
        important of a new group of Washington-based con-
        servative think tanks, policy institutes, political mag-
        azines, lobbies, and other bodies devoted to corpo-
        rate regime change.

1973   Paul Weyrich, the New Right firebrand and tire-
        less organizer, founded the American Legislative Ex-
        change Council (ALEC) to lead conservative initia-
        tives at the state level. ALEC originally was con-
        cerned with issues of abortion and school prayer but
        quickly evolved into a focus on corporate concerns
        as large companies began pouring money into the
        council. ALEC drafted bills such as the "Private
        Property Protection Act," and it helped business in-
        troduce more than 3,100 bills during 1999 and 2000
        alone in state legislatures.

critical launching phases of the corporate social movement, which could be called "Justice for Billionaires."

If you didn't think corporations could become a social movement, think again. Corporations, working individually and through trade associations, began networking into numerous coalitions for specific legislation and ideological campaigns, whether for deregulation or against global warming initiatives. Corporations such as Enron joined scores of such coalitions, including Americans for Fair Taxation, Business Council for Sustainable Energy, Direct Access Alliance, and others promoting procorporate aims.[9]

The New Right regime change reflected the orchestrated efforts of America's biggest corporations, who understood, as Powell put it in his Chamber of Commerce memo, "The day is long past when the chief executive officer of a major corporation discharges his responsibility by maintaining a satisfactory growth of profits. . . . If our system is to survive, top management must be equally concerned with protecting and preserving the system itself."[10] The transformation of corporations into a social movement was the key to regime change, and it turned the Republican Party itself into a movement fueled by the money contributed by companies as well as by the Bible Belt tele-preachers. The movement flourished because of the vast money available, the commitment of the corporate elites, and the insurgent New Right organizers' skill at exploiting new technologies. Viguerie was the mastermind of political direct mail, which became a spectacular tool of educating the grass roots and raising money. The Bible Belt preachers, such as Pat Robertson and Jerry Falwell, whom Viguerie and Weyrich helped persuade to get politically involved, used Christian television and electronic ministry as a remarkable political apparatus, mixing fundamentalism and conservative populism to raise spectacular amounts of money for the cause.[11]

THE NEW DEAL AS SOCIAL ACTIVISM

The same intoxicating brew of fiery grassroots social movements and insurgent policy elites (though lacking the money and organization of the corporate elites themselves) transformed the Democratic Party in the early 1930s. Who were some of these movements?

Communists
Labor organizers
Socialists
Tenant organizers (for the evicted and homeless)
Welfare activists
Wildcat strikers

These groups and hundreds of others took to the streets, providing an angry populist base banging on the door of the Democratic Party. The most important political organizers to arise in that era were labor leaders such as John L. Lewis and Walter Reuther, who galvanized industrial workers from Michigan to Pennsylvania to New York and forced Roosevelt to open the party to working stiffs who had never had a voice before.

At the same time, a new breed of Left-liberal policy wonks and intellectuals, such as Louis Brandeis, Frances Perkins, Harold Ickes, and Henry Wallace, were crafting radical schemas for Social Security, for the Wagner Act legalizing unions, and for all the other landmark legislation of the New Deal. This insurgent intellectual class damped down the raw radicalism of the popular movements. But it created a vision and policy agenda for a regime-changing Democratic Party infused with a people's passion for social justice.[12]

CAN TODAY'S DONKEY AND ELEPHANT BECOME SOCIAL MOVEMENTS?

Today, both parties have become highly professionalized, funded by big business and detached from the people. In an era of normal politics this trend would not be surprising, but at a time of serious structural crisis and emerging regime change, it is historically anomalous, largely reflecting the crisis in the Democratic Party. As economic problems intensify, social movements are proliferating in the country—from the peace movement protesting the invasion of Iraq to the antiglobalization movements exploding on the streets in the 1999 Battle of Seattle and popping up at the summits of trade ministers and financial elites ever since. We are witnessing an era of intense grassroots activism, raging against corporate flight abroad, tax cuts for the rich, service cuts for the middle class and poor, media consolidation, destruction of the environment, erosion of civil liberties, and the wars in the Middle East.[13]

As in the 1970s, the movements are exploiting technology to expand their reach and network themselves into a major political force. Today's equivalent of Richard Viguerie's direct mail revolution and the fundamentalist preachers' televangalizing among the 1970s New Right is the Internet revolution of the peace and justice movements, beginning to seep into mainstream political campaigns, such as that of Howard Dean in 2004. As I show in

Chapter 9, the Internet is proving to be one of the most radical political instruments in history, opening the possibility for social movements without financial resources to make a massive impact on the country and the regime. In the hands of movement activists, it has become one of the great threats to the regime, and corporate money cannot destroy or silence it. The rise of MoveOn.org, a group that mobilized hundreds of thousands of protestors over the Internet to challenge the war in Iraq and has since engaged in numerous other progressive campaigns, is perhaps the most striking example of the generation of electronic activists.[14]

The anomaly is the continuing disconnect between the movements and the Democratic Party establishment. As the contradictions of the regime deepen, the mainstream Democrats continue to practice normal politics, although Howard Dean got an initial surge because he connected with the anger of some of the movements. The mainstream Democratic establishment resists the movements, claiming that they alienate the NASCAR dads and soccer moms in the mainstream. But in fact the movements express the needs of precisely these working family constituencies for regime change. The Democratic establishment has failed to see that it is only in normal politics that the Independents and so-called center are best recruited by the move to the middle. In regime change politics, as the populist best-selling author and former Texas Commissioner of Agriculture, Jim Hightower, titled one book, "There's Nothing in the Middle of the Road But Yellow Stripes and Dead Armadillos."[15] By the way, if you want to learn more and have a really good time doing it, check out Hightower's latest book, *Thieves in High Places*.[16]

RULE 4: IT'S ALL ABOUT CREDIBILITY

Just like you and I, regimes age over time—and the afflictions that will eventually destroy them become increasingly severe. Politicians playing by the normal rules paper over the crises, pretending they will go away or don't really exist (think of the current regime's approach to global warming or Iraq). As the contradictions intensify, *the explanations and remedies offered by leaders become less honest and plausible and create a regime crisis of credibility.*

In U.S. corporate regimes, as noted earlier, such credibility crises are endemic, stemming from the fact that the regimes proclaim themselves to be democratic but serve the interests of financial elites. Corporate regimes have credibility problems even in their early phases because of this inherent gap between democratic rhetoric and practice. As is evident today, the credibility problem worsens over time as recessions, job loss, debt, and other economic problems mount.[17]

Credibility crises in failing regimes are both systemic and personal. Systemic credibility crises involve erosion of faith in the basic institutions of society. Antonio Gramsci called the systemic version in capitalism a *crisis of hegemony,* when people no longer have faith in the corporate order. Enron is a mini-example of a hegemonic crisis, bringing into question faith in the markets even among the investor class that gets the payoffs.[18]

Regime change politics is fueled by systemic credibility crises, with insurgent movements seeking to expose the regime's fundamental deceptions and awaken the public to the need for a more credible order. The nineteenth-century Populists who challenged the robber baron regime mounted the most radical challenge to the credibility of a corporate regime in U.S. history. They made a powerful case that the Rockefellers and Morgans were fleecing the country, impoverishing the majority of farmers and immigrant workers and lying about the corruption and greed that lay at the heart of the regime. The Populists ultimately failed but laid the groundwork for the progressive reforms under Teddy Roosevelt that eventually toppled the robber baron regime.[19]

A THUMBNAIL HISTORY OF CREDIBILITY CRISES

The New Dealers didn't have to work that hard to challenge the 1920s corporate regime's credibility. After the 1929 market crash, systemic credibility melted away with the Great Depression. Nonetheless, corporate leaders continued to proclaim that the corporate order could heal itself, and Roosevelt had to wage a major campaign to discredit these claims. The establishment of the New Deal became a bloody battle of credibility between Roosevelt and the conservative corporate establishment. Roosevelt won only because he was tenacious, aligned himself with mass popular movements, and made alliances with powerful sectors of the business elite itself. Ultimately, he successfully undermined the credibility of the old order because it had collapsed so spectacularly in the Depression and could no longer paper over its own failures.[20]

The New Righters had to wage a similar credibility battle against the declining New Dealers in the 1970s. The New Right learned from Populists of the 1890s, embracing its own rhetoric of populism and calling for a people's crusade against big government rather than against big business. The New Right won the credibility battle that the nineteenth-century Populists lost, because the New Deal was collapsing in the 1970s under the weight of an energy crisis, a major recession combining high unemployment and skyrocketing interest rates, and a shifting balance of power from government to corporations fueled by globalization and "The Revolt of the Bosses." And the right-wing Populists had access to the huge coffers of the corporate elites, while the 1890s Populists were dirt-poor.

Credibility crises are personal as well as systemic. As systemic crises intensify, political leaders have to personally make claims about regime viability as the regime begins to unravel. Toward the middle and late phases of regimes, presidents and other regime leaders typically get ensnared in a web of lies, deceptions, and misrepresentations essential to covering over the crises and maintaining the credibility of a failing regime. When a credibility crisis gets personal, and the president's own credibility is compromised, the endgame of the regime may be approaching.

The combination of systemic and personal credibility crises creates a lethal combination, giving rise to the politics of *bad faith*. The politics of regime change becomes a battle over the bad faith of the regime, and the regime cracks when the personal credibility of the president erodes along with the systemic credibility of the leading corporate institutions. As we see in the following chapters, bad faith has become endemic to the current regime, and a politics of regime change is emerging and moving toward a climactic struggle of credibility.

ANSWERS TO NAME
THEIR GAME (P. 74)

Bush Sr., Clark, Clinton, Gephardt, Gore, and Kerry all play normal politics (Gore had a slight shift, as discussed). Kucinich, Nader, Reagan, and Roosevelt play(ed) regime change politics. Interestingly, George W. Bush and Howard Dean are ambiguous cases. Dean's "campaign for change," initiated after he withdrew from the 2004 presidential campaign, aimed to shift the Democratic Party closer to a regime change mode of politics. By bringing millions of new voters into politics and creating an electoral movement to "return the country to the people," Dean was the mainstream Democratic candidate most closely attuned to regime change issues. He played an important role in awakening the Democratic Party to the need to shift its game from normal to regime change politics.

PART II

Extreme Regime

*T*he next five chapters of the book are mainly devoted to a discussion of President George W. Bush, the fourth president ruling the current corporate regime. Bush is the most extreme face of the regime. Under Clinton and even under Bush's father, a more benign façade masked the underlying realities. But Bush has ripped off the mask and shown the regime's true colors. Analyzing Bush the younger in some detail is a way to see the regime with all the lights on.

I focus heavily on the harm inflicted by Bush and the broader regime on the nation. In both global and domestic affairs, the third corporate regime has caused agonizing and lasting damage to people, the environment, and democracy itself. A clear-eyed view of the Bush administration reveals the underlying extremism of the larger regime it has inherited and makes clear that the regime is now laying the groundwork for its own demise, following short-sighted policies that fuel horrendous economic and social crises that will doom the regime over the long haul.

The regime has maintained popular support through a political culture of "bad faith," involving serious and multiple lies and deceptions. While some of these lies have been discussed widely in the media and in other books, I approach them differently. I show they are part of a broader ideological campaign to legitimate not just Bush but a corporate regime in power since 1980. My aim here is to demonstrate that the regime cannot survive without bad faith, and that Bush's deceptions—about war and the economy—are long-standing features of a regime that needs to mislead and divert its own citizens. The regime's preoccupation with regime changes abroad is a natural and inevitable consequence of the need to forestall movements for regime change at home.

I focus on Bush not only because he offers a window to expose the regime's extremism and bad faith, but also because defeating Bush is a crucial way to weaken and, ultimately, put an end to the third corporate regime. Because Bush is carrying out the regime's unvarnished agenda, defeating him would send a strong message that something is fundamentally wrong with the regime itself, and that Americans are ready for a change. If Bush wins in 2004, it will cement the current regime politically but will not solve its underlying systemic crisis. A second Bush term could lead toward an irreversible economic decline and a more intense military repression at home and abroad to contain popular unrest. In the end, this could produce a right-wing regime replacing the third corporate regime. It would look even more like the Brave New World that George Orwell feared. It might not happen, but one thing is clear. The economic crises stoked by the regime itself are sure to bring it down eventually, whoever wins in 2004.

CHAPTER 4

MARRY YOUR ENEMY

They didn't do everything they could have before 9/11 to prevent the tragedy that was 9/11. [The Clinton team] built a plan [to dismantle al Qaeda] and turned it over to the Bush administration. This administration failed to do its duty to protect the United States of America before 9/11.[1]

GENERAL WESLEY CLARK, *January 12, 2004*

MEET BEVERLY ECKHART

Beverly is the wife of Sean Eckhart, who was killed in the World Trade Center on 9/11. On August 8, 2003, at an event commemorating the anniversary of the nuclear bombing of Nagasaki by the United States, Beverly spoke to a group in Nagasaki.

"On September 11, 2001, my husband, Sean, called me from the 105th floor of the World Trade Center. The fates, in their mercy, granted us enough time to say what we needed to say to each other before the building collapsed and he was carried to his death."

> *Beverly has joined a group called September 11 Fami-*
> *lies for a Peaceful Tomorrow. The group is speaking out*
> *vigorously against the president's war on terrorism. It ar-*
> *gues that events leading up to 9/11 have been covered up,*
> *that the military response by President Bush is going to in-*
> *cite more terrorism, and that the police, fire fighters, and*
> *other "first responders" are being underfunded.*
>
> *Beverly says, "On September 11, 2001, America was*
> *thrust into sisterhood with countries and peoples she had*
> *once helped, as well as countries and peoples she had once*
> *hurt." In other words, the United States has inflicted on*
> *others what it suffered on 9/11. Beverly is concerned that*
> *fear not be exploited to incite more aggression under the*
> *cloak of false accusations or lies. Her central plea at Na-*
> *gasaki was that "we must, above all, demand integrity*
> *from those who govern us politically."*

In this chapter and the next, I show that today's regime can survive only by practicing a foreign policy of bad faith that I call "marry-your-enemy." Since we live in a world of *Oprah,* think of this as a codependent marriage. In such a marriage, the two partners may hate each other but, at the same time, cannot survive without each other or without the war between them. They become dependent on the "enemy" for their very existence. Our current regime suffers from the same condition: it has a codependent relationship with its own enemy.

"Whoa!" you may say. "We have been mainly discussing domestic issues and suddenly here are monumental claims about foreign policy. This is a big shift." Yes, you are right, but the foreign and domestic policies of a regime are intertwined. This chapter and Chapter 6 shift our focus temporarily to foreign affairs, a matter especially important to a global corporate regime. I will soon show how tightly connected war and foreign policy are to the daily crises of our workers and to the prospects for regime change at home.

Well, what kind of foreign policy does a corporate regime practice? One that suits the needs of its corporate patrons. And corporations require, above all else, *expansion,* to secure new markets, new resources, and the cheapest labor on the planet.

It is hardly surprising, then, that expansionism has been at the heart of U.S. foreign policy since the first corporate regime. It came easily to a country that loved the idea of "Manifest Destiny" and always had a messianic belief that its values should guide the world. Don't you remember studying Manifest Destiny in grammar school—and believing in it? Though they did not control the regime, corporations had enough power to help propel an expansionist foreign policy even in the Progressive and New Deal Eras, partly exploiting the nation's messianic greed.

Today's corporate regime has an appetite for expansion like none before it. Its insatiable hunger to control the entire planet is something new, and it reflects the rise of the transnational corporation. Unlike the corporation of earlier regimes, today's corporation must compete in a global market and is wired like a global Pacman: it must gobble up other parts of the world or die. What was once a preference for expansion becomes a core survival imperative on a grand scale. The long-standing corporate appetite for expansion morphs into a *systemic need for global empire,* a core pillar of the current regime discussed in Chapter 1.

Now, this creates a serious problem for the regime, because no American government can say openly that it has a foreign policy based on controlling the world. To admit this would be to admit you are in violation of international law, that you don't believe in the democratic right of other countries to govern themselves, and other obviously bad things. Even an American president cannot openly state such things!

The solution to this regime-threatening conundrum presented itself in the form of international adversaries that threaten not only the regime's interests but also, potentially, the security of ordinary Americans themselves. The regime mobilized itself to defeat these enemies, knowing all the while that the war against the "enemy" is also a way to advance and explain its global pursuit of power. And the regime saw an exceedingly important fringe benefit: the war provides the political recipe at home for a regime that is increasingly undermining the well-being of its own citizens.

Marry-your-enemy can be seen as a foreign policy game of this regime with the following rules:

Identify a credible enemy that is evil.
Pursue global power in the name of defeating the
evil enemy.
Rely on fear of the enemy as a charmed way to
survive politically at home.

From the time it was born, the regime survived by adhering strictly to the rules of this foreign policy game. In the next section, I show how, at the outset of the regime, President Reagan created a codependent relationship with the Communist enemy he tried to destroy. I then show how

President Bush now seeks to sustain the regime by creating exactly the same utilitarian relationship with the terrorist enemy he hates. In both cases, the pattern repeats itself: the enemy allows the regime to claim to defend its own population and the larger world by seeking American dominion over it. In Chapter 5, I show that the same pattern is the key to the regime's political survival at home.

Two caveats. While this sounds like a conspiracy theory, it is not. I am not suggesting that regime leaders invented Communism or terrorism (though U.S. policies helped give rise to al Qaeda), or that they don't really want to destroy the enemy. The United States has faced real threats, and Reagan and Bush have both no doubt been sincere in their hatred of the Soviets and al Qaeda. But this has not stopped these presidents from hyping the threat or relying on the enemy for the vast political benefits the regime can reap in fighting them.

Second, I am not suggesting that the practice of politically exploiting your enemy is unique to this regime—or even to corporate regimes in general. Great empires from Rome to Britain have often propagated bad faith about war and enemies, claiming to defend and civilize those they conquered. In America, manipulation of the enemy in the Cold War preceded the current regime, which has no monopoly on deceptive foreign policy games. But the current U.S. corporate regime has a far more acute and systemic need to play the marry-your-enemy game. Because of its extreme imperatives, this regime has exploited the notion of a global crusade against evil spectacularly, perfectly tailoring it to a global corporate order unprecedented in scale and ambition.

BAD FAITH AT BIRTH: THE REGIME
AND THE EVIL EMPIRE

Eminent journalist Bill Moyers produced a 1987 PBS documentary, *The Secret Government,* focused on the Cold War and the Reagan years. In it, a dairy farmer from Wisconsin said that he and his friends used to talk about "slick people" such as used car salesmen and lawyers. But now, he said, "We talk about the liars." He meant the politicians in Washington, and he meant the president.

Moyers's film focused on the Iran-Contra scandal that unfolded under President Reagan. Reagan created a guerrilla, terrorist army of Nicaraguan mercenaries, called "Contras," to overthrow the Nicaraguan government, using U.S. funds diverted secretly from illegal sale of missiles to the Ayatollah in Iran. During the Iran-Contra congressional hearings, Oliver North, Reagan's chief aide in the scandal, declared straight-out: "Yes, I lied to the Congress." And he admitted lying to the American people—but he had no qualms. Lying, he said, is necessary since it is in the interest of protecting Americans. What he didn't say was that the lying was really necessary to protect the president and the corporate regime—not the people!

The regime formed around a central "big lie" linked to the Cold War *that wed U.S. leaders to the Communist enemy.* This grand deception was inherited from an earlier regime, but Reagan honed it until it was a master ideology and essential prop of the new regime. Reagan came to power by promising to rid the world of the evil of Communism, and the war against evil has been the master ideology of the regime ever since.[2] Reagan hated the Soviets, but he came to rely overwhelmingly on the Cold War to pursue his imperial global foreign policy and to survive politically at home. He needed his Communist enemy more and more even as he sought more frantically to destroy him.

I recently showed Moyers's film to a Boston College class and asked my students to write down a gut reaction. I then went around the room and asked what they wrote. One student said *"betrayal."* Another cried out *"disgust."* A third whispered *"sad."* A fourth said *"outrage."* A fifth hissed *"anger."* A sixth said *"shocked."* And so it went. These few words were repeated over and over by all eighty students in the class.

I do this exercise every year, and the students always respond the same way. What the students react to so emotionally is not just Oliver North's lies but the unexpected message about the Cold War as bad faith: a reliance on the Soviet enemy to achieve unstated and unacceptable aims. Moyers shows that Reagan intervened in Nicaragua, El Salvador, and other countries, *always claiming to fight Communists but often acting to secure American corporate interests, whether in bananas or in cheap labor.* In the name of anti-Communism, he propped up brutal dictatorships that opened their countries to plunder from abroad and committed terrible crimes against their own people. The methods: covert CIA intervention, military and financial aid to dictators, direct military intervention, torture and assassination efforts, putting LSD in Fidel Castro's cigars.

As soon as the regime was born, starting with Reagan and continuing with his successors, the regime routinely intervened to support corporate-friendly dictators, always using the Soviet enemy as the justification.

Reagan and Bush, Sr., often *did* intervene to counter

BORN TO INTERVENE

Afghanistan 1980s United States supports Islamic
   fundamentalists, such as Osama bin Laden,
   to overthrow Soviet-allied government

El Salvador 1980–93 United States supports Salvadoran
   "death squad" regime famous for killing Archbishop
   Romero and Jesuit priests

Guatemala 1980s United States supports dictators
   killing and torturing thousands of indigenous
   Guatemalans

Haiti 1980–87 United States props up terrorist dictator
   Baby Doc Duvalier

Honduras 1980–90 United States supports terrorist
   dictators

Indonesia 1980s United States sends billions to
   support dictator Mohamed Suharto

Iraq 1980s United States sends aid to Saddam Hussein,
   long on the CIA payroll

Libya 1981–89 United States tries to assassinate
   the dictator Moammar Qaddafi

Nicaragua 1980–90 United States supports terrorist
   "Contras" in violation of U.S. Boland Act

Panama 1989 United States overthrows Noriega,
   the dictator it long supported

The Philippines 1980s United States props up dictator
   Ferdinand Marcos

South Yemen 1979–84 United States supports covert,
   illegal regime change[3]

what they saw as a Soviet threat, but in many cases the Soviets had nothing to do with it. There was no Soviet threat
in Iraq through the 1970s and 1980s when we supported
Saddam even as he gassed his own people, that's for sure!
Nor was there a Communist enemy in Honduras, Indonesia, Guatemala, Grenada, Panama, or Haiti, to name just
a few. In these countries, a Soviet threat was invented or
hyped because the regime needed to intervene for less noble aims. Cheap labor and profits abroad are the lifeblood
of a global corporate regime, but you can't tell the world or
the American people that is why you are sending the troops
to overthrow foreign governments or install notorious dictators.

In the film, Moyers gets close to talking about marry-
your-enemy. He shows that while the conflict between the
United States and the U.S.S.R. was real enough, the American regime turned the Soviet Union into an extremely useful adversary, justifying regime aims that could not be
openly discussed. The new U.S. regime sought to secure a
global corporate market, defined as "the free world"—and
if it took dictators to pacify the local population or beat
them into submission, so be it. The United States wished
the Soviet Union would go up in smoke, but as long as it existed, the American corporate regime developed a fruitful
partnership with the enemy. Our favorite dictators could
be called allies in the war against Communism rather than
tyrants. The Cold War was a gift from God to the American corporate regime, allowing violent repression of na-
tionalist or worker movements (think of the Nicaraguan
Sandinistas) to be redefined as a war against Communism.

The Soviet enemy was exceedingly useful to the regime
in domestic politics as well. As soon as the regime formed

The Cold War was a kind of tacit arrangement between the Soviet Union and the United States under which the U.S. conducted its wars against the Third World and controlled its allies in Europe, while the Soviet rulers kept an iron grip on their own internal empire and their satellites in Eastern Europe—each side using the other to justify repression and violence in its own domains.[4]

NOAM CHOMSKY

in 1980, the elites had to find ways to persuade Americans that their hard-earned taxes should support corporate welfare rather than the social needs of the U.S. population. The Cold War created an American population living in terror of the "Evil Empire," distracted from a domestic agenda that involved brutal corporate downsizing and massive social cuts.

THE ODD COUPLE: WHY BUSH NEEDS BIN LADEN

Bush and Osama bin Laden already have their own partnership, one that serves the same purposes for the U.S. regime as did Reagan's marriage to the Soviet enemy. I am not really just thinking about bin Laden, nor of the long, intriguing history of business collaboration between the Bush and bin Laden families that Michael Moore and other critics are bringing to light.[5] No, the problem is systemic and independent of the personalities involved, and it clearly is a replay of the marry-your-enemy game practiced by Reagan.

Islamic terrorists of all stripes give Bush (or any other regime leader) the ideal enemy to justify his pursuit of corporate empire and to rally political support for the regime at home. Bush gives bin Laden and al Qaeda *their* perfect enemy to justify terror and recruit young men and women. Pax Americana and Islamic terrorism, each seeking to destroy the "pure evil" of the other, become increasingly dependent on each other in their war to the death, fearful that outright victory over the codependent enemy would destroy their own raison d'être.

The most important benefit for Bush is in domestic politics, since he would have great difficulty winning reelection in 2004 without al Qaeda and other terrorists to fight. Political exploitation at home of the war on terrorism is so central that I have made it the exclusive subject of Chapter 5. For now, though, I focus on how the terrorist enemy has become an indispensable partner to a regime pursuing a global corporate empire.

THE BUSH REVOLUTION
FROM THE HORSE'S MOUTH

The impetus to global domination is so strong in the Bush administration that members of the administration are speaking frankly about a Bush "foreign policy revolution." For example, Richard Haas, Bush's Director of Policy Planning in the State Department, explained:

> You might call [the Bush doctrine] the limits of sovereignty. Sovereignty entails obligations . . . not to support terrorism in any way. If a government fails to meet these obligations, then it forfeits some of the normal advantages of sovereignty, including the right to be left alone inside your own territory. Other governments, including the U.S., gain the right to intervene.[6]

In veiled language, Haas is making the regime's case for extending U.S. sovereignty over the rest of the world, i.e.,

American empire. Haas declares, "In the case of terrorism, this can even lead to a right of preventive self-defense. You essentially can act in anticipation if you have grounds to think it's a question of when, and not if, you're going to be attacked," precisely President Bush's argument for the invasion of Iraq.[7] The current regime thereby begins to disenfranchise global citizens and whole countries, which find their control of their lives eroding as rapidly as that of displaced American workers at home.

As discussed in Chapter 1, empire is one of the great pillars of this regime. The third corporate regime has always wanted to bring the entire world into an integrated global market and security system under U.S. control. This policy preceded not only Bush but the regime itself, ramping up after World War II when American leaders realized that the Europeans could no longer run the world. But because transnational companies are now the driving force, and global profits trump everything else, the rush to empire became far more important in the current regime. With his foreign policy revolution, Bush has jammed the gas pedal down to the floor, but the same road map has guided all current regime leaders, starting with Reagan and followed by both Bush's father and Clinton.

CAPITALIZING ON TERRORISM: DECEPTION NUMBER 1

Beyond its domestic political uses, the war on terrorism is now based on *three* other basic deceptions that together constitute bad faith and put on clear display a dedicated commitment to playing the marry-your-enemy game. The first involves use of the terrorist enemy to expand and justify a global corporate empire after the Soviet enemy disappeared. The collapse of the Soviet Union created jubilation and then near panic among regime planners. It removed the greatest remaining deterrent to U.S. global dominance, but gone also was the justification for American global control.

U.S. leaders thrashed around for a replacement national security creed to justify empire. Some trial balloons that just couldn't do the job were floated about, mainly during the Clinton years:

> Global drug war
> Stop rogue states
> Humanitarian intervention
> Prevent ethnic conflict
> Rebuild failed states

The regime needed heavier ammunition for a serious policy of empire, and the terrorist threat began to be floated. But in the 1980s and 1990s it was still a long shot: despite repeated attacks on American ships and embassies, the terrorist threat was not particularly credible as a substitute for the Evil Empire.

But 9/11 changed that immediately. In a widely discussed interview with *New Yorker* journalist Nicholas Lemann, Bush's National Security Advisor, Condoleezza Rice, said, "There is a big global threat . . . shifting the tectonic plates in international politics. And it is important to try to seize on that and position American interests . . . before they harden again." In the same interview, she told Lemann that she had called together her staff right after 9/11 to ask, *"How do you capitalize on these opportunities?"*[8]

It is no secret what opportunities regime leaders had in

mind. They were outlined more than ten years ago by a team led by then Secretary of Defense Cheney in the Bush, Sr., administration, well before the war on terrorism. A series of documents trace the regime plan that 9/11 finally made possible.

1992 Under Bush, Sr., a U.S. national security team chaired by Dick Cheney pronounced a grand American strategy "for maintaining U.S. preeminence, precluding the rise of a great power rival."[9] The report called for overwhelming U.S. power to prevent any other nation from even imagining it could challenge U.S. control. Presented to Bush, Sr., in a private briefing by Paul Wolfowitz and later leaked to the *New York Times*, the report stirred sharp criticisms about unilateralism and American imperialism.[10]

1997 Neoconservatives founded the Project for a New American Century (PNAC), a school for future Bush administration policy officials. PNAC issued a torrent of reports about the need to invade Iraq.

2000 PNAC issued a report, "Rebuilding America's Defenses," reaffirming the 1992 Cheney strategy document. Issued a year before 9/11 and nine years after the collapse of the Soviets, the new PNAC report declared, "At present the United States faces no global rival. America's grand strategy should aim to preserve and extend this advantageous position as far into the future as possible."[11]

September 11 finally made the wheels turn. The Cold War was over, but the regime now had a permanent war on evil—a stunningly useful enemy partner—that could justify unilateral intervention anywhere on the planet.

The war on terrorism involves a second basic form of deception: selectively and hypocritically defining "terrorism." The regime focuses only on those forms of terror that the United States deems counter to its own interests, and it disguises the forms of state terror that the United States itself has supported throughout the regime. The simple truth is that a state with a historical record of supporting terrorist dictators cannot credibly lead a war on terrorism, reinforcing the bad faith at the very heart of the current regime. Our regime leaders have supported some horrific rulers in large measure because they deliver the goods that the transnational corporations crave: cheap labor and the freedom to operate without any inconvenient labor or environmental standards. And regime leaders have gotten away with it only because there was an enemy—a greater evil—who justified it all.

In a tape made by John Stockwell, a senior CIA officer in the 1980s, Stockwell tells about being present, along with other CIA officers, in a room where a political prisoner was being tortured. They were in a U.S.-sponsored military regime in Latin America. The torturers were part of the government's internal security service, which has had a long working relationship with the CIA.

Stockwell describes how electrodes were applied to the genitals of the person being tortured. The CIA officers, such as Stockwell, did not apply the electrodes or administer the electric shocks themselves, but they were watching and occasionally offering advice. The CIA agents were dressed in suits with ties, and the atmosphere was casual, with officers joking around a bit. At one point, a phone call for one of the CIA officers from his wife was put through. As electric shock was being applied to the naked person on the table, he said, "Oh, hello dear, I'll be a little late tonight. I've got to finish up a few more things at the office." "It's all very civil and part of a good day's work," Stockwell comments drily.[12]

Stockwell is only one of several CIA insiders to report U.S.-sponsored torture and other forms of state terrorist behavior during the Cold War. In the 1980s, the regime, always in the name of fighting the greatest evil, Communism, militarily and financially supported states that practiced torture, including:

El Salvador: The United States advised and observed torture sessions administered by the Salvadoran National Guard.

Guatemala: The CIA advised Army Unit G-2, whose techniques included electric shock, cutting off limbs, and burning flesh.

Honduras: The United States supplied notorious Honduran Battalian 316, including shock and suffocation devices.

Panama: United States soldiers tortured Panamanian forces after the 1989 invasion, including one case of a metal cable shoved into a prisoner's open wound.[13]

If you think the United States has stopped supporting states that practice torture, think again! Read the 2003 *Amnesty International Report*,[14] which describes torture practiced by these United States allies, in the Americas alone:

Argentina
The Bahamas
Belize
Bolivia
Brazil
Chile
Colombia
The Dominican Republic
Ecuador
Guatemala
Guyana
Haiti
Jamaica
Mexico
Paraguay
Peru
St. Lucia
Trinidad
Venezuela

State terrorism around the world, operating with the knowledge or complicity and assistance of the U.S. government, has flourished in this regime until the present day, the most damning form of bad faith now corrupting the American war on terrorism—but one integral to the marry-your-enemy game. After 9/11, the United States increased aid to many brutal and often terrorist regimes, such as Pakistan, bringing under its wing countries infamous for brutal violence against their own populations. In the name of the war against terrorism, the United States, according to Amnesty International and other sources,[15] has been rewarding allies who are some of the world's worst state terrorists. *These are friends of Bush you should know about.*

Since 9/11, for example, the United States has been sending troops and funds to the oil-rich country of Uzbekistan, in return for use of its airfields as a staging ground in the war against the Taliban in Afghanistan. President Bush has given strong new support to President Islam Karimov, notorious for his use of torture, censorship, and repression of any opposition parties. Karimov is known to have thrown in jail and tortured a man just for wearing a beard. A Communist Party boss when Uzbekistan was part of the Soviet Union, Karimov jails or murders those who oppose his regime, calling them Islamic terrorists. While there have been extremist Islamic movements in his country, Karimov applies the same brutal tactics to democratic dissidents. The Bush administration applauds Karimov as an important ally in the war on terrorism, and it has more than a little interest in his oil fields.[16]

One of my students is doing her senior honors thesis on the United States relationship to Uzbekistan, and she reported some of these facts to a class I teach on U.S. foreign policy. You could hear a pin drop in the room when she spoke. Students were deeply confused and distressed that the United States is supporting a state terrorist regime in the very name of the war against terrorism.

One student said that she does not see how the United States can credibly lead any kind of war on terrorism given what it is doing in Uzbekistan. Another said he is not sure state terrorism is the same as al Qaeda terrorism, but he is nonetheless troubled and puzzled. A third student wondered whether "terrorism" is just a scare word that the United States pins on a country when it turns against U.S.

interests. A fourth said he believes that the United States is acting in justifiable self-defense, but he acknowledged that the United States is violating some of its own moral absolutes. A fifth student said that the whole legacy of state terror makes the U.S. war on terrorism a lie. How can the United States claim to wage a war against terrorism, she wanted to know, when it has been complicit in decades of state torture and murder of civilians in places like El Salvador or Uzbekistan?

The students would be even more alarmed by Amnesty International's conclusion that the United States is fighting terrorism by getting more intimate with many countries, such as Uzbekistan, that are themselves state terrorists practicing torture, illegal detention of prisoners, and abuses of human rights, typically in the name of the war on terrorism. Among those singled out in the 2003 *Amnesty International Report* are many U.S. regime allies:

> Colombia
> The Congo
> Egypt
> Georgia
> Israel
> Pakistan
> Saudi Arabia
> Tajikistan
> Uzbekistan
> Yemen

We need a global campaign against terrorism, but it will be a charade until the United States cleans up its own act. The United States could best end terrorism abroad by ceasing its own support of it. But it will continue to support such regimes because 1) the terrorist enemy allows U.S.

regime leaders to support them with impunity—oh, how useful an enemy can be, and 2) these regimes tend to deliver the business-friendly environment that the corporate patrons of the regime desire, especially when it comes to oil!

BROCCOLI, OIL, AND BAD FAITH: DECEPTION NUMBER 3

I asked a foreign policy class of one hundred students how many of them believed that the United States would be sending troops to Iraq and other Middle Eastern countries if the region were a broccoli field instead of an oil field. Nobody raised his or her hand.

This is the third form of bad faith made possible on a new scale now—the most obvious way in which the evil enemy splendidly serves the aims of the regime. The core countries in which the United States is now focusing its military expansion in the name of the war against terrorism contain the biggest reserves of oil in the world, including the huge, recently discovered reserves around the Caspian Sea. The quest for control of Mideast oil is not new with Bush or this regime, but its importance in the global corporate regime is unprecedented.

Nearly every major nation to which the United States has sent significant troops or intensified its military and political focus since 9/11 is an important oil producer or a site for crucial pipelines. They include Colombia, Georgia, Indonesia, Iran, Iraq, the Philippines, Tajikistan, Uzbekistan, and Yemen.

Hello! Is this any surprise to you? We are sending troops into oil-producing countries where U.S. global companies have long craved a direct U.S. presence. Thanks to the terrorist enemy—again—for making possible this prized regime aim!

The quest for oil, backed up by our need to fight the enemy, underlies and explains the most important and often perplexing moves the United States is now making around the world. It makes sense of why the United States remains the major military and political sponsor of Saudi Arabia, the world's leading oil nation, which produced fifteen of the nineteen infamous September 11 hijackers and whose clerical establishment has helped promote the radical Islamic anti-American doctrine breeding terrorism through the entire region. Russia's gradual integration into the grand American military alliance against terror is driven by the fact that Russia possesses the largest oil reserves outside the Middle East; that makes it the obvious alternative to Arab oil should catastrophe strike in the Muslim world.

But the marry-your-enemy game is complex, and things are not quite so simple in the war on terrorism as "blood for oil." Iraqi analyst Rahul Mahajan notes, "Although oil is the primary consideration in U.S. Middle East policy, it is very far from true that oil companies determine that policy."[17] United States support

Undoubtedly, a primary reason for the attack on Afghanistan is the installation of a regime that will oversee an American-owned pipeline bringing oil and gas from the Caspian Basin, the greatest source of untapped fossil fuel on earth and enough, according to one estimate, to meet America's voracious energy needs for 30 years. Such a pipeline can run through Russia, Iran or Afghanistan. Only in Afghanistan can the Americans control it.[18]

JOHN PILGER, *journalist*

of Israel has drawn fire from oil companies who fear a backlash from Arab governments. Additionally, U.S. sanctions on Iraq in the 1990s hurt U.S. oil companies seeking Iraqi oil deals.[19] The United States does not always seek cheap oil prices since it is a large producer of oil itself, and U.S. foreign policy is not focused on access to oil per se because oil is traded on the world market and the source is not all-important. In fact, the United States tries to get most of its oil domestically, and increasingly from Latin America and West Africa. These reservations are important, particularly the recognition that the foreign policy of this most corporate of regimes is not always driven by corporate executives or seen as serving their interests.

Despite these important caveats, oil nonetheless helped drive the Iraq war and the broader war on terror in major ways:[20]

Oil in Iraq and other Islamic states is "a material prize," giving U.S. companies greater control over the region's oil development.

It is a "political lever" that will make it easier for the United States to counter OPEC control over the global oil supply.

It helps secure the dollar as the global reserve currency, preventing it from shifting toward the euro, as it might if European companies had greater control over Iraqi or Caspian oil.

It helps the United States ensure a larger global supply of oil at a time of growing domestic and global demand.

Exploitation of the regime's prized terrorist enemy to secure oil obviously involves bad faith. And—no surprise—it speaks to what this regime is ultimately all about: profits for Exxon, Texaco, Bechtel, and America's other greatest global corporations.[21]

CHAPTER 5

DOG-WAGGING WITH BUSH

*T*he popular film *Wag the Dog* portrayed a president who invented a war in a faraway place to distract attention from domestic scandal that could destroy his presidency. While this plot might have seemed tailor-made for President Clinton during Monica-gate, President George W. Bush has his own domestic problem, which I call *Econogate* in Chapter 7. How does he paper over a huge gap between his whole domestic agenda and the will of the American people? Polls show that the majority of the people feel the regime is going in the wrong direction on almost every issue—indeed, that the domestic agenda is directly counter to their own interests.

Hollywood provided the answer to Bush's domestic problems. His advisors have promoted the war on terror as if they were scriptwriters for *Wag the Dog*. Mark McKin-

WRONG TURN

Job creation
Debt and fiscal responsibility
Environmental protections
Social Security
Education
Trade
Corporate welfare and scandals
Energy policy and global warming
Poverty
Inequality

non, Bush's chief media advisor in the 2000 campaign, said after 9/11 that homeland security and the war on terrorism throw "a huge blanket over the entire domestic agenda. The domestic agenda right now is security. It's covering up everything else."[1] Only a tad more circumspect, Matthew Dowd, chief pollster for the president, said regarding the merits of the war on terror, "Issues that the Democrats may have an advantage on may get shoved aside, like the environment or Social Security."[2] The president's chief political advisor, Karl Rove, has been laser-focused on the virtues of the war on terror, shoring up the GOP base while capturing suburban Independents who might defect if the campaign focused on domestic concerns.

In Chapter 4, I showed that the marry-your-enemy game is a strategy to disguise the pursuit of empire as a war against terrorism. In this chapter, I show the game is even more important as a strategy for winning elections at home. *This regime, and particularly President Bush, could not politically survive without marrying the terrorist enemy.*

DOG-WAGGING AS SURVIVAL

Unfortunately for Bush, the "domestic problem" will not go away, because it is rooted in the regime's fundamental corporate identity. The S & L, junk bond, and other financial scandals of the Reagan era, and the election of Clinton, failed to weaken the growing corporate stranglehold over Washington. In 2000, transnational energy corporations bankrolled Bush's victory in the GOP campaign as well as his general election. For 2004, they did it again, with gusto!

The resulting domestic agenda is tailored to the prayers of American big business. It's hard to believe, and to stomach, that the Bush administration boasts the list of "accomplishments" in "Payback Time."

The administration has launched a brazen assault on American democracy, not to mention a blunt attack on white-, pink-, and blue-collar workers, all victims of downsizing, outsourcing, lower wages, slashed benefits, and broken social services. The soccer moms and NASCAR dads are in peril, as are the Reagan Democrats in the Midwest and the entire bloc of suburban Independent voters Bush needs.

The 2002 Enron crisis exposed the systemic cronyism of the Bush administration and created acute political problems. Bush called the problem "a few bad apples," but even business magazines, such as *Fortune,* called the problem "systemic."

PAYBACK TIME

The Bush administration can take credit for the following historic maneuvers:

Passed a radical tax-cutting agenda awarding 90 percent of its returns to the top 1 percent of taxpayers and awarding huge depreciation allowances, overseas exemptions, and other loopholes to the biggest global corporations

Supported trade policies freeing service-sector companies, as well as manufacturing companies, to move abroad and slash jobs at home

Increased subsidies to agribusiness, fossil-fuel and nuclear energy, and military and high-tech firms

Opened up national parks and other federal lands to exploitation by timber, coal, and other companies

Appointed commissioners to the Securities and Exchange Commission and the Federal Trade Commission who were cronies of the industries they were regulating and known enemies of regulation itself

Appointed commissioners to the Federal Communications Commission who openly stood for deregulation of the mass media and telecommunications industries they were supposed to police

Lowered or repealed environmental standards, including those on clean air and water

Slashed spending on transportation, child care, welfare, job training, public housing, and most other social welfare programs

Launched a wave of anti-labor appointees to the National Labor Relations Board

*Over the past months,
the public has been
treated to an ever-
lengthening parade
of corporate villains,
each seemingly more
rapacious than the last.
. . . But, by now, with the
feverish flush of the new
economy recognizable
as a symptom not of
a passion but of an
illness, it has also
become clear that the
mores and practices that
characterize this greed
suffused the business
world far beyond Enron
and Tyco, Adelphia
and WorldCom.*[3]

FORTUNE, *September 2, 2002*

With his presidency and the survival of the regime itself potentially at stake, Bush responded with tough talk about corporate responsibility, new disclosure rules, and jailing corporate criminals. But his credibility was severely compromised by his long association and obvious coziness with a corporate world run amuk with greed. His appointment to Chair of the Securities and Exchange Commission of Harvey Pitt, a former lawyer for huge accounting firms who quickly became a major embarrassment and was forced to resign, did not help. Nor did revelations that President Bush, as a director at Harken Energy, and Vice President Cheney, as CEO of Halliburton, were linked in the 1990s to insider dealing and accounting "misstatements" resembling those at Enron and WorldCom. Bush's personal and financial link to Enron CEO Ken Lay—who contributed more to Bush's lifetime career than any other funder—didn't help matters, either.

The historic crisis of confidence in corporate America loomed, then, as a threat to the entire regime, and as a particularly dangerous and personal threat to Bush's political prospects. Let's be blunt: a sustained public focus on En-

MORE THAN A FEW BAD APPLES

The country's most respected companies, such as GE, Xerox, and Disney, were forced to acknowledge "accounting misstatements," and prestigious financial giants, such as Citigroup, Morgan Stanley, Merrill Lynch, Bank of America, and Goldman Sachs, were indicted in a mushrooming, systemic conflict of interest that has discredited corporations, accounting firms, banks, and brokerage houses. Markets went into free-fall, the dollar sank as foreign investors began to lose faith in American securities, and the entire credibility of corporate America and the financial markets was called into question. Clearly, the problem was the barrel, i.e., the regime, not a few bad apples.

ron and other domestic issues clearly presaged a political train wreck for Bush and the regime. Less than two years later, the major 2003–2004 scandals at Putnam Investments, Strong Investment, and scores of other mutual funds made the problem even worse. Bush had to divert voters' attention as quickly as possible from the financial scandals, the jobs meltdown, and the exploding deficits, a tall order for which the war on terrorism seemed ideally suited.

Wag-the-dog is the name of the game corporate regime elites must play with terrorists to overcome their little "domestic problem"; it is the way that marry-your-enemy works in domestic politics.[4]

The 2002 midterm elections were a textbook case of wag-the-dog, a model that worked so well it became the obvious guide to Bush's 2004 strategy. Whereas Franklin Roosevelt told Americans that the "only thing we have to fear is fear itself," Bush took an opposite approach, working to increase Americans' fear as a way of focusing their attention on the threat, essentially shouting, "BE AFRAID!"

In the summer of 2002, the administration came out with nearly daily warnings of new threats and terrifying possible plots, whether of dirty radioactive bombs or of bridges that might be blown up in New York or San Francisco, or of attacks on nuclear power plants. Reports of threats against the symbolically compelling Statue of Liberty or July Fourth celebrations, as well as warnings of biological, chemical, and nuclear attacks on American cities, became staples of speeches by Bush and his leading cabinet officials. Any of these horrifying things might actually have happened, but the warnings did little to help prevent them, serving mainly to heighten popular fear and the psychological need to invest faith and authority in the president. The distribution of potassium iodine pills to people living in the shadow of nuclear power plants was reminiscent of the exercises during the McCarthy era of children being drilled to hide under their desks in the event of a nuclear attack.

Republicans argued that it was unpatriotic for anyone to portray the war on terrorism as a political strategy to re-elect the president, and for many months after 9/11 it was a subject the media didn't touch. But in the summer of

2002 as congressional elections approached, the White House intensified a campaign to draw attention to the continuing terrifying threats and to the country's need to stay intensely focused on the war. Defense Secretary Donald Rumsfeld warned repeatedly that terrorists equipped with nuclear, chemical, and biological arms would attack us. Bush made nearly every public announcement an occasion to remind Americans of the need to be "patient, steadfast, and focused" for a "long war" against "pure evil," keeping the public's attention on terrorism as elections approached. Bush himself joked that maybe he "talked war" just a bit too much, and Chris Matthews, host of MSNBC's *Hardball*, suggested on July 2, 2002, that the president "knock it off." Important as the terrorist threat was, Matthews said, we had known far worse in World War II, the Depression, and other, bigger calamities.

Republicans continued to charge that anyone who linked the war to politics was undermining the war effort, but they quietly acknowledged the enormous political utility of the war. When the Department of Homeland Security was announced, conveniently timed to divert attention from embarrassing revelations that the administration had failed to "connect the dots" before 9/11, Bush aides denied any political calculations in any aspect of the war on terrorism, but then they acknowledged to persistent reporters that it was part of an electoral strategy. Asked as early as 2002 about the Bush campaign theme in 2004, Karl Rove allowed that he liked one idea circulating among Republican strategists: "Are you safer now than you were four years ago?"[5]

Cut to May 1, 2003, right after the cessation of "major hostilities" in Iraq. In what is widely seen as the debut of Bush's 2004 campaign, Bush donned military gear, boarded a military fighter plane, and landed on the *Abraham Lincoln,* one of the giant naval antiaircraft carriers in the Persian Gulf. Taking off his helmet and striding across the deck like a figure out of *Top Gun*, Bush seemed the ultimate warrior against terror. A large poster on the deck read "Mission Accomplished." With photographers positioned strategically to capture the moment, the photo of Bush as terrorist terminator was flashed all over America, reappearing so many times that it became almost iconic. Rove had successfully launched the 2004 campaign in the spirit of the 2002 model.

On September 8, 2003, as the presidential campaign was heating up, Bush addressed the nation about the deteriorating situation in Iraq. The Democrats had just launched the campaign season with their first major primary debate, in which all nine candidates lambasted the president for the millions of jobs he had lost. With large flags on both sides of him and a small one on his lapel, Bush opened by saying, "I have asked for this time to keep you informed of America's actions in the war on terror." What followed was a defense of his presidency as "rolling back the terrorist threat to civilization."

Bush compared his war on terrorism, and U.S. occupation of Iraq, to America's historic actions after World War II. He was telling Americans to vote for him because he was the true heir to the "greatest generation," which had saved America in World War II. "Following World War II, we lifted up the defeated nations of Japan and Germany and stood with them as they built representative governments . . . America today accepts the same challenge. . . . And for America, there will be no going back to the era before September 11, 2001 . . ."

While this was not officially designated a campaign speech, Rove was rebranding his product, George W. Bush, as a historic wartime president. Poll watchers in the administration calculated that every move drawing attention to the war and to Bush as commander-in-chief sustained his popularity and prospects for electoral success. With the capture of Saddam Hussein a few months after Bush's speech, the war strategy for reelection got a huge boost. But the president had to make clear that the war against terrorism was not over and that victory required a heroic Roman gladiator warrior—Bush would be Russell Crowe in the White House. The president incessantly reminds Americans that the terrorist dangers have not passed, suggesting we are engaged in a war of destiny requiring his own towering leadership. This became the foundation stone and mantra of his 2004 reelection campaign.

THE BLOGS GET IT

On the hundreds of "blogs," or personal websites, devoted to the 2004 elections, there is endless talk of dog-wagging. Says one blogger, commenting on the Republican convention to renominate the president planned for New York City in early September 2004:

> We all know why this is. . . . It has a close chronological relationship with September 11th. . . . the GOP con-

vention is to be held in New York City as a lead-in to
September 11th remembrance festivities. I can see the
video montage now:

> People crying, bleeding, and running as a building
> collapses.
> Fade into Bush on top of a pile of rubble, rallying
> workers.
> Fade into Bush addressing a joint session of Congress.
> Back to live feed of Bush walking from backstage. . . .
> taking the microphone from his introducer, Nancy
> Reagan, and say[ing,] "We STILL stand united."[6]

Declares another blogger:

> Bush can't be defeated unless his credibility as com-
> mander-in-chief is eroded. The sad truth is, he's good
> at lying, or to use Maureen Dowd's well-turned phrase,
> "the Orwellian fan-dance." He's gonna wag the dog un-
> til Hell won't have him.[7]

It's hard to put it better. Much of the public has caught
onto wag-the-dog. But heightened orange alerts, airplane
security delays, and Bush's constant pronouncements
about looming threats have kept too much of the public in
terror. We Americans should remind ourselves and George
W. Bush of FDR's full statement about fear in his 1933 inaugural address: "The only thing we have to fear is fear itself—nameless, unreasoning, unjustified terror which par-
alyzes needed efforts to convert retreat into advance."

CHAPTER 6

THE PERFECT STORM

It was all about finding a way to do it [take out Saddam]. That was the tone of it. The president saying, "Go find me a way to do this . . ." Day One, these things were laid and sealed.[1]

PAUL O'NEILL, *Bush's first Secretary of the Treasury, describing a National Security Council meeting just days after Bush entered the White House in January 2001*

On July 15, 2003, soldiers from the Third Infantry Division, a major combat division in Iraq celebrated for its heroism, created a unique kind of storm in the desert. It started after Defense Secretary Donald Rumsfeld said on July 14 that the troops weren't going to be able to come home in September as previously promised. The soldiers and their wives felt as if they were "kicked in the guts, slapped in the face." They had been lied to about the war, and the lies were destroying them. Listen to some of their reactions:[2]

"They've bald-faced lied to us."—Julie Galloway, the wife of a sergeant

"If Donald Rumsfeld was here I'd ask him for his
resignation." —Specialist Clinton Deitz

". . . it pretty much makes me lose faith in the Army."
—Private Jayson Punyhotra

"It feels like we're forgotten, like we fell off the planet."
—Specialist Sean Gilchrist

"We're exhausted. Mentally and physically exhausted
to the point that someone hoped they would get
wounded so they could go home. 'Hey shoot me,
I want to go home.'" —Sergeant Eric Wright

"My solution for President Bush and Donald Rumsfeld
and all those people is just keep your mouth shut.
If you don't know the truth, don't say anything at all."
—Tasha Moore, the wife of a captain

Exposing the president's lies and distortions in Iraq is a
first step in exposing a regime crisis that I call "the perfect
storm." I have lifted this phrase from the book and movie
of the same name, about a once-in-a-generation storm off
Cape Cod, that happened only because of the simultane-
ous occurrence of many extremely unusual weather conditions. The perfect storm, as I am using it here, is about
a once-in-a-generation *political unraveling* that brings together in one explosive event the unseemly realities and
lies of the regime in such a way that the regime itself may
be swept away.

How do you recognize a political perfect storm? Well, it
has two essential features:

It requires "the mother of all lies," deceptions so politically explosive that they destabilize the regime.

It deepens underlying economic and political structural
crises of the regime that cannot be patched.

I show in this chapter that both of these turbulent elements are brewing in Iraq. In Chapter 7, I show that another storm is brewing around the domestic economy. Either one could result in a perfect storm, and together they are this regime's worst nightmare, exposing its deepest vulnerabilities and terminal crises. You will soon see why regime change at home—the subject of the final part of this book—is not only possible but inevitable.

REMEMBER VIETNAM

If you doubt that a war can become a regime-threatening perfect storm, think back to Vietnam. It not only led to LBJ's decision to abandon his quest for a second term, but also triggered the beginning of the end of the New Deal regime. It had both elements of a perfect storm.

The lies that helped destabilize the New Deal regime include the following.

The 1964 Tonkin Gulf deception that got us into the war.
The false mantra—"the light at the end of the tunnel"
—implied a short war although the United States had no exit strategy.
Misleading body counts were provided, and enemy attacks were underreported.
The U.S government claimed that our ally, South Vietnam, had the support of its people.
The U.S. government claimed that South Vietnam was a legitimate state (it was legally supposed to be reunited with North Vietnam in 1956 elections that the United States helped abort).
The U.S. government denied that it was a civil war.

The crises that the regime could not weather politically include the following.

America was driven into fiscal deficits, subverting the regime economy.

The war divided America.

The war bred hatred of Americans among the Vietnamese—revered Buddhist leaders committed suicide by burning themselves to death to protest American policies.

The unilateral war created tensions with allies while breeding anti-Americanism around the world.

Today, monstrous lies once again paper over policies that are illegal, immoral, and politically untenable. And we see again a war without end that could unravel the regime economically and has already disastrously divided the United States internally, as well as pitting the regime against the world. The Iraq war could undermine the credibility of the regime's national security ideology and overburden its economic foundation. The capture of Saddam Hussein, new Iraqi elections, and other short-term developments may appear to solve the Iraqi problem, but they can't and won't. If Bush wins in 2004 it will be based on short-term illusions. An Iraqi perfect storm still will be whistling down on us, whether it is Bush or his successor in the White House.

DO YOU BELIEVE SADDAM HUSSEIN CAUSED 9/11?

If you believed the president and his men, you would probably say yes, you think Saddam helped plot 9/11. According to an October 2002, poll, 66 percent of the American public believed that Saddam was involved in causing 9/11.

They trusted Bush when he said in his 2003 State of the Union address that Saddam Hussein aided and protected terrorists, "including members of al Qaeda." They put faith in his October 7, 2002, talk to the nation, when he said that Iraq's connections with al Qaeda went back a decade. They relied on Secretary of Defense Donald Rumsfeld when he told reporters on September 26, 2002, that the evidence connecting Saddam and bin Laden was "bulletproof." They listened to Condoleezza Rice, National Security Advisor, when she said a day earlier that there were "clearly contacts between al Qaeda and Iraq [and] some of the contacts [were] important." And they believed White House officials who announced the two most important specific connections yet: that captured al Qaeda operative Rafed Fatah underwent training in Iraq, and that a meeting took place between Mohammed Atta, the lead hijacker on 9/11, and an Iraqi agent in Prague in April 2001.[3]

BUSH LIED: LISTEN TO THE CIA, FBI, AND NSC

Millions of Americans took to heart what the president and his men kept saying of the relationship between Iraq and September 11, but CIA and other intelligence officials dismissed the connections as absurd, and the White House knew it. No CIA or FBI report before or after the invasion has documented a working relationship or organizational tie between Iraq and al Qaeda. In a direct contradiction of Rumsfeld's assertion of a "bulletproof" connection, a 2002 CIA report to the Senate Intelligence Committee claimed that any evidence of such ties was "inconclusive." Daniel Benjamin and Steven Simon, staff members of the National Security Council (NSC) from 1994 to 1999, closely examined nearly a decade's worth of intelligence, and they wrote in 2003 that the "religious radicals of al Qaeda and the secularists of Baathist Iraq simply did not trust one another or share sufficiently compelling interests to work together."[4] Benjamin, director of counterterrorism at the National Security Council, said flatly, *There was no noteworthy relation between al Qaeda and Iraq. I know that for a fact.*[5]

Czech President Vaclav Havel, a U.S. ally, and his intelligence service refuted the claim that Atta and an Iraqi agent had met in Prague, forcing U.S. officials to acknowledge that they had no evidence of it and that phone records strongly indicated Atta was somewhere else at that time. A U.N. group researching al Qaeda ties reported finding no links between Iraq and al Qaeda as of June 2003.[6] The British intelligence report that President Bush used as reference for his claim that Rafed Fatah was trained at an al Qaeda camp in Iraq mentioned no such thing. Nor had it ever been documented by any other source.

Investigative journalists Robert Dreyfus and Jason Vest show that in Bush's first National Security Council meeting, within days of Bush being sworn in, members of the council discussed invading Iraq. Led by Paul Wolfowitz, number 2 man at the Pentagon, and Douglas Feith, number 3 man, in late 2001 the Bush administration established a secret intelligence unit in the Pentagon to discredit CIA and NSC intelligence reports and to fabricate an Iraq–al Qaeda link. The unit was run by David Wurmser, a longtime fanatical advocate of regime change in Iraq who had close ties to Richard Perle, Wolfowitz, Feith, Dick Cheney's chief of staff Lewis "Scooter" Libby, and other heavyweight neoconservative regime elites. Its mission was to discredit CIA intelligence reports and *create* intelligence to prove "what did not exist,"[7] i.e., the Iraq–al Qaeda connection. Wurmser had close relations to Ahmad Chalabi, founder of the Iraqi National Congress, an Iraqi exile group, and he relied on bogus reports of links to al Qaeda provided by Chalabi associates. Vincent Cannistraro, a former CIA chief of counterterrorism, described the operation as "progaganda. Much of it is telling the Defense Department what they want to hear, using alleged informants and defectors who say what Chalabi wants them to say [and creating] cooked information that goes right into presidential and vice presidential speeches."[8]

OH, NOW HE TELLS US!

On September 17, 2003, Bush finally acknowledged, "We have no evidence that Saddam Hussein was involved with the September 11" attacks.[9] The president's statement disputed almost two years of the administration's assertions to the contrary. It also raised constitutional questions about his written statement to Congress on March 18, 2003, when he declared invasion of Iraq. In that statement he wrote that the United States was acting under Public Law 107-243, which authorized U.S. intervention against "those nations, organizations, or persons who planned, authorized, committed, or aided the terrorist attacks that occurred on September 11, 2001."[10] His acknowledgment that the United States had no evidence of Iraqi participation suggests that the president violated U.S. law.

Bush's administration was filled with zealots who had been pushing for Iraqi regime change even in their previous roles under Bush, Sr., and Clinton. After 9/11, Bush decided to take Saddam out, but the intelligence data were still too soft to support even a weak case for invasion based on connections to al Qaeda. Bush thus hyped the thinnest evidence of any ties into definitive claims and concealed from the U.S. public the negative thrust of intelligence coming from the CIA, the FBI, and others around the world.

WHERE ARE THE WEAPONS OF MASS DESTRUCTION?

A second set of regime-threatening deceptions about Iraq became iconic across the world as weapons of mass destruction (WMD) remained nowhere to be found. Instead, it's clear that the U.S. regime has amassed a vault of weapons of mass *deception*.[11]

1) **THE LIE:** President Bush said in his 2003 State of the Union message (SOU) that "Iraq recently sought significant quantities of uranium from Africa." The president referred specifically to "yellowcake uranium that Saddam had allegedly sought from the West African country of Niger."

THE FACTS: As early as March 2002, the CIA repeatedly told the White House and vice president's office that this claim was dubious and based on forged documents, and the White House removed it from previous speeches. CIA Director George Tenet fell on his own sword and took responsibility for the "misstatement," as did a White House speechwriter, but not before the yellowcake uranium story had turned into the single lie most widely reported and discussed by major U.S. newspapers and television stations.

2) THE LIE: On the Sunday before the war, Vice President Cheney said, "We believe [Saddam] has, in fact, reconstituted nuclear weapons."

THE FACT: In January 2003, the International Atomic Energy Agency (IAEA) flatly contradicted this statement in its report to the U.N. Security Council, finding "no evidence that Iraq has revived its nuclear program since the elimination of the program in the 1990s."[12]

3) THE LIE: On September 8, 2002, Secretary of State Colin Powell told Fox News that there was no doubt that Saddam had chemical weapons stocks.

THE FACT: A September 2002 report from the Defense Intelligence Agency said, "There is no reliable information on whether Iraq is producing and stockpiling chemical weapons."

4) THE LIE: In his 2003 SOU, Bush said that Iraq "has attempted to purchase high-strength aluminum tubes suitable for nuclear weapons production."

THE FACT: The IAEA told the U.N. Security Council that the tubes were not designed or usable for nuclear weapons, a view shared by the State Department and Defense Intelligence Agency.

5) THE LIE: On March 30, 2003, Secretary of Defense Rumsfeld said that the administration "knows where [Iraq's WMD] are. They are in the area around Tikrit and Baghdad and east, west, south, and north somewhat."

THE FACT: No WMD have been found in that area or elsewhere in Iraq.

6) THE LIE: On May 30, 2003, Bush said, "We found the weapons of mass destruction. We found biological laboratories." On June 1, 2003, Bush said, "We found a biological laboratory in Iraq."

THE FACT: U.S. and U.K. experts found this claim false, saying that some mobile trucks identified by Colin Powell as bio labs were carrying food seed, and the lab that Bush referred to was used for the production of hydrogen for weather balloons. No evidence of biological labs has been found.

7) **THE LIE:** In his 2003 SOU, Bush said, "Iraq had the materials to produce as much as five hundred tons of sarin, mustard, and VX nerve agent . . . and has given no evidence that [it] has destroyed them."
THE FACT: U.N. inspectors had concluded that by 1998 Iraq had destroyed at least 95 percent of its chemical weapons. Iraq claimed in its report to the United Nations that the rest had degraded and pointed to areas where this had happened. U.N. inspectors acknowledged that these materials would degrade and that trace elements in the areas referred to suggested Iraq's claim was true. No chemical weapons have been found.

The record of lies and distortions about WMD is so vast that it has produced an explosion of media and Internet reports, although the media have focused almost exclusively on the yellowcake uranium lie. Rumsfeld himself implicitly acknowledged the pattern of deception when he told the Senate Armed Services Committee—after the war, on July 9, 2003—that the United States invaded not "because we had discovered dramatic new evidence of weapons of mass destruction. We acted because we saw the existing evidence in a new light—through experience on 9/11."[13] While not highlighted by the media, Rumsfeld's admission was a bald contradiction of the Bush and Blair administrations' main claim of a *new and imminent* threat from WMD based on *new* evidence, warranting a preemptive attack in self-defense. The WMD lies, notorious in Britain, created a political firestorm that seriously weakened Blair. The same could happen to Bush. On January 26, 2004, David Kay, Bush's hawkish chief of U.S. weapons inspector in Iraq who searched for WMD for nine months, resigned. He concluded about Saddam's WMD, "I don't think they exist."[14] The increasing tranparency of the WMD lies stripped away the "moral clarity" of the war on terrorism and shook the political ground under the regime.

WHEN THE WHITE HOUSE LEAKS

The yellowcake lie became even more politically explosive after White House officials leaked the name of a CIA agent, Valerie Plame, the wife of senior U.S. diplomat Joseph Wilson, a former ambassador to Iraq. The disclosure of Plame was made to columnist Robert Novak and six other journalists by two senior White House officials, but it was only Novak who published it on July 14, 2003.[15] This alleged "outing" of a CIA agent, the first in fifty years by White House officials, was a crime endangering her life and threatening U.S. intelligence sources. It is widely viewed as retribution for Wilson's exposure of the yellowcake lie. In a July 6, 2003, *New York Times* op-ed piece, Wilson made public that he had personally investigated for the U.S. State Department, at the request of the vice president's office, allegations of the Iraqi effort to purchase uranium ore, and he had told the administration that it was an obvious fabrication.[16] On October 1, 2003, President Bush assured the country that the Justice Department would "do a good job" in finding the individual who leaked, but a rising chorus of Democrats and national media called for an independent investigation. The CIA leak highlighted both the gravity of the administration's lies about WMD and the lengths the administration was willing to go to punish those who investigated or exposed them.

Even Bush's own Justice Department has acknowledged that these lies are serious and may involve criminality, by appointing a special prosecutor to investigate the CIA leak. But beyond the political damage to Bush, the whole pack of WMD lies have become so notorious internationally that they threaten the credibility of the regime's foreign policy. If people believe the United States intervened under false pretenses in Iraq, they will become skeptical about future U.S. wars. This puts into doubt the regime's ability to pursue empire—whether under Bush or another president—which is essential to the survival of the regime itself.

NO EXIT: THE QUAGMIRE THAT COULD SINK A REGIME

A third set of regime-threatening lies and deceptions, this one about the ongoing occupation of Iraq, could prove to be the most damaging, not just for Bush but for regime presidents who follow him. The most important deception, as in Vietnam, involves the administration's failure to tell Americans that the war may have *no exit*. Prior to invasion, Bush said that troops would remain in Iraq "not a minute longer than necessary," implying that the occupation would be mercifully short. But the truth is that the U.S. military

is already planning for a multiyear occupation, and nobody in the regime has an exit strategy.

The realities of a quagmire are beginning to trickle out. The number of U.S. troops killed since Bush declared "mission accomplished" has been greater than during the so-called war. By the fall of 2003, Americans were hearing about soldiers dying daily in scores of attacks, but they still weren't getting the full story. Veterans for Common Sense and other groups accuse the administration of concealing a far larger number of attacks on American soldiers than that reported in the press, attacks that seriously wounded thousands of soldiers.[17] In November 2003, the new U.S. commander finally declared a state of "guerrilla" war, a co-ordinated, intensifying pattern of attacks by Iraqi civilians against coalition troops with no end in sight.

The bombing of the U.N. headquarters in October 2003; the multiple suicide bombings in Baghdad and other Iraqi cities throughout the fall and winter of 2003; the October 26, 2003, attack on the Al-Rasheed Hotel in Baghdad when Deputy Defense Secretary Paul Wolfowitz was in the building; the killing of two U.S. soldiers in Mosul on the six-month anniversary of the occupation; the Black Hawk military helicopters shot down in November 2003; the spectacular Baghdad attacks on Christmas, 2003—all suggested that the Bush administration had either tragically miscalculated, or not leveled with the public about, the postwar realities of chronic war.

Disinformation about the cost of a long war has already become a political vulnerability for Bush. With deficits sky-high, the administration acknowledged to Congress in July 2003 that the cost of the occupation was $3.9 billion every month and could go much higher. Both Democrats and Republicans in Congress complained that the administration was stonewalling about the real long-term cost, which likely will mount into the hundreds of billions of dollars. Initially, Bush and other top administration officials had suggested that Iraq's oil revenues would pay for reconstruction. Later, however, they acknowledged that those revenues would barely pay for the modernization of the dilapidated Iraqi oil industry itself.

As costs mounted, Bush requested $87 billion for Iraqi occupation and reconstruction for the 2004 fiscal year. Both liberal and conservative Americans wondered why the administration was pouring billions into an occupation in Iraq when initiatives ranging from Head Start to Homeland Security were being underfunded at home. On October 31, 2003, after Congress reluctantly approved Bush's request, the Defense Department issued an estimate—a scary Halloween surprise for American voters—that the costs of the occupation *on top of this request* could range from $85 billion over four years to $200 billion over ten years, even if there were sharp reductions in U.S. forces. This, itself, is clearly a gross underestimate, since the cost was already $166 billion before the end of 2003.[18]

IRAQ'S LIBERATION: DÉJÀ VU

The precedent for the perfect storm brewing in Iraq is what happened to Britain when it invaded Iraq in 1917, and you need to know this history if you doubt any of my claims about a deceptive, endless war that could bust the regime. The British troops captured Baghdad on March 11, 1917, and the British commander, Major General Stanley Maude, bellowed to the Iraqis: "Our armies do not come into your cities and lands as conquerors or enemies but as liberators." What followed was a forty-year occupation and resistance culminating in a coup against a British puppet regime in 1958.[19]

General Maude was not telling the truth. The British were there to occupy for the long term rather than to liberate. Their aims were to dominate the Middle East as the Ottoman Empire crumbled, to take over trade routes to India, and eventually to control the newly discovered Arab oil fields. The British War Minister, Lord Kitchner, wanted to set up a British proxy caliph, Hussein ibn Ali, to be the British base in the region, and although Iraq gained formal independence in 1931, the Brits ran a puppet government until the 1958 coup.

Resistance to British occupation broke out almost immediately, and by 1920 a low-intensity guerrilla war was churning, with 425 British deaths. In the London *Sunday Times,* on August 22, 1920, T. E. Lawrence—Lawrence of Arabia—said that the British public had been led "into a trap from which it will be hard to escape with dignity and honor." Lawrence wrote that the public had been "tricked into it by a steady withholding of information . . . The Baghdad communiqués are belated, insincere, incomplete. Things have been far worse than we have been told, our administration more bloody and inefficient than the public knows." He concluded, "We are today not far from a disaster."[20]

The parallels to today are eerie. Bush is repeating the British disguise of occupation as "liberation." The U.S. occupation has already triggered a guerrilla resistance similar to the one faced by the British in 1920. A long, costly occupation, linked to a puppet Iraqi regime, is virtually certain. The United States will keep U.S. forces in Iraq for years after it turns over formal control to a client Iraqi government.

Both wars reflect an underlying imperial thrust. As it was for the British, the most important American interest is establishing strategic control of the Gulf region. Just as the crumbling of the Ottoman Empire opened this window for the British, the collapse of the Soviet Union made possible the neoconservative dream of reshaping Iraq as part of a U.S. imperial order in the entire Islamic world, an aim that almost certainly will inflame the whole region and generate long-term resistance in Iraq itself.

The other motive for the war that the administration does not acknowledge is U.S. control of oil (in Chapter 4 I explain the complicated interest the regime has in Mideast oil). The British had the same goal, using their occupation to secure control of Iraqi oil by British firms that dominated Iraq for half a century. The U.S. Agency for International Development (US-AID) has begun to reward U.S. oil companies through a closed bidding process. Halliburton, the Texas-based oil giant formerly headed by Dick Cheney, was awarded the first major contract for servicing Iraqi oil wells and for fire prevention in the oil fields, estimated to be worth $7 billion. In the third quarter of 2003, Halliburton announced that Kellogg, Brown, and Root (KBR), its subsidiary in Iraq, had increased its revenue to $2.3 billion from less than $1 billion the prior quarter, and it had more than doubled its profits in its Iraq operation. (Some of the profit was based on fraud and kickbacks that KBR acknowledged in January 2004.)

Of course, it's not only oil the regime is interested in. In 2003, U.S. Administrator in Iraq Paul Bremer issued decrees ensuring that Iraq would be "open for business" to all U.S. companies. Here are the most important orders—Numbers 12, 37, 39, and 40—all probably in violation of international law, according to a secret memo prepared by the British Attorney General, Lord Goldsmith, for British Prime Minister Tony Blair:[21]

BREMER ORDER NUMBER 39—FOREIGN INVESTMENT

All Iraqi industries (other than oil, banks, and insurance, which are covered separately) were ordered to be privatized and open to 100 percent foreign ownership, with unrestricted rights of investors to remit all funds and profits, and with forty-year contracts. This means not only Iraq's water and electrical systems, but also its farms, factories, and telecommunications, could be 100 percent foreign-owned and -operated.

BREMER ORDER NUMBER 40—BANKING

The Iraqi banking system was immediately privatized by allowing foreign banks to own 50 percent of any Iraqi bank. Bremer awarded J. P. Morgan Chase—implicated in the Enron crisis—the contract to run a consortium called the Trade Bank of Iraq.

BREMER ORDER NUMBER 37—TAXES

A flat 15 percent tax was implemented for corporations and individuals, so rich Iraqis and corporations will pay the same tax rate as the poorest Iraqi slum dweller.

BREMER ORDER NUMBER 12—TRADE LIBERALIZATION

Most custom duties, import and export surcharges, and other fees are now required as a way of integrating Iraq into the corporate-friendly rules of the World Trade Organization (WTO).

CHENEY'S SHAME

A congressional investigation concluded that Dick Cheney's relationship to Halliburton posed a conflict of interest and violated federal ethics standards, since Cheney, with 433,000 Halliburton stock options, still receives compensation from the firm, including $205,298 in 2001 and $162,392 in 2002.[22]

Such orders are evidence of the regime's intent to integrate Iraq into its global corporate design. Iraq's resources are protected not for Iraqis, but for foreign firms.

THE VIETNAM SYNDROME

I started this chapter with references to Vietnam because that war was a quagmire that helped bleed an earlier regime to death. Iraq is the same kind of regime-threatening quagmire because of the clash between U.S. regime aims and the democratic desires of the Iraqi people. *Let us be clear about why this regime cannot leave Iraq, even though by staying it risks undermining itself economically and politically, as it did in Vietnam. It is because the regime does not want what the Iraqi people want, and it must keep U.S. soldiers on the ground for years to maintain control.*

The regime wants a unified federal Iraqi state allied with U.S. corporate interests. But what do the Iraqi people want? Each of the three primary ethnic groups in Iraq has its own desires and interests. Generally speaking, the Kurds in the north of Iraq have wanted their own state for more than a century. The Shiites, Iraq's 60 percent majority living mainly in the south, want control of some form of Islamic republic. They seek close relations with Iran, with whom they share historic, religious, and tribal bonds. But Iran is on the American "axis of evil." The Sunnis, in the Baghdad area, want to retain their privileges gained under Saddam Hussein. Some wish Hussein were back in office, many are irrevocably hostile to the United States, and most fear domination and retaliation from the Shiites.

To put it bluntly, the Iraqi people do not share a common interest with either today's U.S. regime or each other. Remember that Iraq was cobbled together by the British after World War I from three separate provinces of the Ottoman Empire. It is a Western construction rather than a creation of the people themselves. (In some ways, the problem is even worse in Iraq than it was in Vietnam because the Vietnamese were ethnically unified and passionately shared the desire to be a single independent nation.) If the United States were to give Iraqis real democracy, they almost certainly would decide on one or more of the following options.

1) A three-state solution: Kurdish, Sunni, and Shiite independent nations, a solution this U.S. regime will not accept.
2) An Islamic republic: a government dominated by the majority Shiite population, which opposes American foreign policy in the region and rejects Western concepts of church-state relations.

3) A federated government: a body unable to reconcile the interests of the three main ethnic groups or to quell the resistance of militants from inside and outside of Iraq. The United States might accept this solution, but it would require major long-term U.S. occupation and turn Iraq into an American satellite, clearly an unacceptable option for the people and the region.

Bottom line: No democratic outcome exists that is both consistent with U.S. regime interests in the region and sustainable without a costly, economically debilitating, permanent U.S. military occupation. The current rhetoric about liberation and democracy is a lie, and the United States is destined to follow the historic trajectory of the British.

The U.S. regime could ultimately be undermined in Iraq; without an exit plan, the war will cost hundreds of billions of dollars and aggravate economic and political crises already mounting in the regime (I discuss these further in the next chapter). The reality of "no exit" also explains why regime leaders must continue to not tell the truth to the American people.

I said at the beginning of this chapter that one way you know a perfect storm is the political

The whole thing [national elections in Iraq projected for 2004] was set up so President Bush could come to the airport in October [just before the U.S. presidential elections] for a ceremony to congratulate the new Iraqi government.[23]

AHMAD CHALABI,
Chair of Iraqi Governing Council and founder of the Iraqi National Congress, November 27, 2003

gravity of the lies it requires. Just how serious are the lies around Iraq? Listen to John Dean, President Nixon's legal counsel during Watergate and one of the most respected Republican elders of the regime.

> In the three decades since Watergate, this is the first potential scandal I have seen that could make Watergate pale by comparison. If the Bush Administration intentionally manipulated or misrepresented intelligence to get Congress to authorize, and the public to support, military action to take control of Iraq, then that would be a monstrous misdeed. . . . To put it bluntly, if Bush has taken Congress and the nation into war based on bogus information, he is cooked. Manipulation or deliberate misuse of national security intelligence data, if proven, could be "a high crime" under the Constitution's impeachment clause.[24]

John Dean is telling us that Bush's are not ordinary lies: they are the once-in-a-generation kind that breed a perfect storm. The Constitution explicitly mandates Congress to investigate "high crimes and misdemeanors," including presidential behavior that could lead to impeachment. Dean argues that to allow President Bush immunity from his lies about Iraq would render moot the most sacred principles that James Madison put into the Constitution about the responsibilities of the legislative branch and the ultimate importance of decisions regarding war.

Iraq's potential to be a quagmire, hidden before the war by a thick cloak of deceptions and likely to continue even after formal authority is turned over to an Iraqi government in 2004, seriously undermines Bush's principal political asset: leadership on national security. But just as important, it puts a severe economic strain on a regime that is in trouble for other reasons that I explore in the next chapter. As with Vietnam, a long war could become the straw that broke the regime's economic back, the most important structural crisis driving a perfect storm.

CHAPTER 7

ECONOGATE

Econ-o-gate (i-'kä-nə-gāt) *n* 1: a series of lies, deceptions and subterfuges aimed to shift economic, social, and other resources away from the public to the elites 2: a government policy perfected during the presidency (2000–2004) of George W. Bush 3: a suicidal survival strategy of the third corporate regime

MEET MARLENE WINGATE

Marlene is fifty years old and has been in the publishing business all of her working life. She started out at a big publisher in the late 1970s and, "within an hour of starting," she says, "part of my job was to develop what is called in publishing jargon 'a stable of freelancers.' As with horses." Ironically, a few years later, Marlene would become part of the stable and work in it even until the present day.

Marlene explains that publishers started outsourcing for reasons common during the Reagan Revolution. It was "one way in which you diminish the size of your staff and undercut the clout of the bargaining unit. It was all about saving money," she says.

I was saving the company enormous amounts of money by developing this stable of editorial freelancers who did all the hands-on work. You know, all of the development, copy editing, proofreading, indexing, the industry was moving towards a system that it now has in which the people on staff were mostly traffic cops working with outside vendors. . . . The companies are making a lot of money not paying benefits. They are able to pay an hourly rate and fee structure that is depressed relative to the cost of living. They don't train workers and don't take responsibility for workers in down times.

Marlene left the big publisher, which she described as "a terrorist environment based on 'institutionalized contempt.' Contempt for the work and contempt for the workers, and a lack of respect for what really were very high-level skills." She was hired by a small publisher and became managing editor, but she was laid off when the company was caught up in a big merger. At that point, Marlene started her freelancing career, sick of the companies and free to "sell my services to various clients, principally textbook publishers. I specialize in big, long-term, messy projects." But there were new problems, associated with downturns, loss of benefits, and lack of bargaining power. She helped organize an association to bring free-

lancers together and force some decent standards on the industry.

Marlene had always wanted to get an advanced degree. She finally got a doctoral fellowship at a major university and started to actualize her real dream. She's now three years into her dissertation and continuing to freelance, but it isn't enough money to live on. The recession, the Bush tax cuts, and the state budget crises are looming big in her life.

Marlene is a realist. She says, "I never left freelancing when I went back to school, and I knew I might never be able to." She'll get her degree, but she thinks she might be back out in the stable with the other horses. Just a horse with a Ph.D.

Econogate is a cover-up of the connections between Bush's economic policies and the mounting domestic casualties. Like Iraq, Bush's domestic economic policies create the conditions for another regime-threatening storm. Recall from the last chapter that a perfect storm involves monstrous lies disguising horrific policies and crises. Econogate is a set of economic policies ruinous to the American people and the regime itself, covered up by huge lies papering over a hellish witch's brew of joblessness and red ink.

Bush is waging a corporate-driven ambush of ordinary Americans that is the domestic counterpart to the "battle of Baghdad," an ongoing campaign for the most radical socioeconomic transformation since the Civil War. The first stage of the war—launched with massive tax breaks for the rich, radical deregulation, vast corporate welfare, zero-budgeting for social programs, and new policies to facilitate corporate flight abroad—is familiar from the Reagan years. But vast casualties have been recently littered all over the home front. The most obvious are the Americans who have lost their jobs; not surprisingly, 50 percent of Americans feel like Marlene and tell pollsters that they fear for their own job in the next year. In August 2003, a Gallup poll found that 81 percent of Americans said it "was a bad time to find a quality job."[1]

Bush's deceptions about his domestic agenda must be exposed quickly, both to save the jobs of tens of thousands like Marlene and to prevent the nation from sinking into irreversible debt and decline. Beyond the truth about the grim future of ordinary workers is the even grimmer reality of a crisis that could lead the country into bankruptcy. In this chapter, as in the last, I explain the mother lies about our economy and the underlying crises that could be disguised right up to November 2004 but that will eventually become apparent as they bring down the regime.

LYING ABOUT THE WAR AT HOME

All corporate regimes engage in covert war against their populations, since their aim is to redistribute wealth and power from the people to elites. President Bush has created a unique and far more explicit pack of lies about the war at home against American workers and communities, and his lies have the wind power of a perfect storm. The deceptions of the president and his lieutenants have been so numerous, shameless, and transparent that they have given a fresh boost to the genre of political satire, propelling books by humorists such as Jim Hightower, Al Franken, Michael Moore, and others to the top of best-seller lists. But laughing is hard going for Marlene and her fellow workers. It is also hard for them to accept their president's promises. And who can blame them? Take a look at just a few examples of Mr. Bush's face-to-face "misrepresentations."[2]

WHAT HE SAID: "I am touched by the kids and the nurses and the docs, all of whom are working to save lives . . . and [will make sure] the health care systems are funded." (visiting Egleston Children's Hospital in Atlanta in March 2001)

WHAT HE DID: Bush's first budget proposed cutting funds to children's hospitals like Egleston by 15 percent, or $34 million, and his 2004 budget proposed cutting another 30 percent ($86 million) from grants to children's hospitals.

WHAT HE SAID: "We've got to do more to protect worker pensions." (addressing workers in Madison, Wisconsin, in August 2002)

WHAT HE DID: Four months later, the Treasury Department proposed highly controversial rules that "would allow employers to resume converting traditional pension plans to new 'cash balance' plans that can lower benefits to long-serving workers." Critics say the rules violate federal law by discriminating against older workers.

WHAT HE SAID: "All you've got to do is . . . watch the pride that they exhibit when they show you the kitchen and the stairs . . . they are so proud to own their own home." (touring the Carver Homes in Atlanta, a subsidized housing development funded under a HUD Hope VI grant, June 2002)

WHAT HE DID: On February 5, 2003, Bush's HUD announced it was phasing out the Hope VI Grant that funds the Carver Homes in Atlanta.

WHAT HE SAID: "... the most important issue for any governor in any state is to make sure every single child in your state receives a quality education." (addressing Rochester Community and Technical College, a vocational education school, October 18, 2002)

WHAT HE DID: His 2004 budget proposes to cut vocational and technical education grants that fund Rochester College and other vocational colleges by 24 percent, or $307 million.

Bush's sneak attack, continuing the battle against workers begun by Reagan at the regime's outset, has already devastated the unemployed and the working poor, who together constitute close to 40 percent of the population. John I. Brown is one of the many long-term unemployed casualties worse off than Marlene. The TRW factory in Cleveland laid him off from his assembly line job fifteen months ago, and he says, "I feel bitter. Every week I send out three or four applications, but it's not easy. Every time I look around, there's another company going out of business or going overseas." Richard Curtin, a survey researcher at the University of Michigan, says "Most workers expect the economy to improve, but at the same time they don't expect to have their income or their wages increase. It's a very untypical environment."[3]

In September 2003, as the economic recovery was said to be picking up, Carl Van Horn, director of the Heldrich Center for Workforce Development at Rutgers University, said, "American workers are doing very badly. All the trends are in the negative direction. There's high turnover, high instability, a reduction in benefits, and a declining loyalty on the part of employers."[4]

A perfect storm paralleling the one brewing in Iraq

could arise from the numbers of casualties of Bush's war at home and the lies that cover up those numbers. An "iconic number" is one that grabs the mind and doesn't let go, such as 59 percent, the fraction of the male average wage earned by the average female worker in the 1970s. That figure became famous as a measure of gender discrimination in the workplace and helped to catalyze a feminist movement. Today, whatever the short-term economic situation might be, the iconic number is the number of jobs lost under Bush—almost certainly between two and three million by the elections in November 2004.

"Bushspeak"—the language of the cover-up—says that the job loss and social crises stem from the costs of the war on terrorism and Iraq, the failed policies of the past administration, and global economic forces outside of Bush's control. But as Harry Truman, a plainspoken president, put it, "The buck stops here." That's especially true of policies that directly hurt you and me.

Cuts in vocational educational programs keep the shrinking middle class from getting the skills for a better job.
Tax subsidies for corporations moving abroad steal jobs out of the country.
Deregulation contributes to accounting scandals and corporate bankruptcies.
Changed pension policies help create retirement nightmares for workers.
Changed overtime policies keep Americans who work extra hours from getting paid fairly.
Tax cuts for the rich remove billions that could be better invested in public schools, health care, and job training.

Beyond the mother lies discussed thus far, Econogate is a cover-up of the regime's long crusade to enrich the wealthy, through wholesale privatization and radical changes in taxes. Beyond the horrendous job policies, the red meat is a series of remarkably radical programs for restructuring the concept of, and taxation of, wealth. Taxation had always been based on a view that wealth is produced from collective human labor and thus should be redistributed in some measure to all who contribute to it. Bush has reconceptualized wealth as the constitutionally protected fruit of pure individual initiative, thus negating the basis for taxing or controlling it.

In the most radical shift since the introduction of the income tax in 1913, Bush has slashed the dividend tax and abolished the inheritance tax while creating astonishing tax shelters for upper-income families. Abolishing the capital gains and dividend taxes will benefit overwhelmingly the top 1 percent, who already control about 40 percent of the nation's wealth and 49 percent of taxable stocks and mutual

TALK ABOUT BIG TAX CUTS!

Based on their own tax statements, President Bush, Vice President Cheney, and their cabinet stand to gain an average of $42,000 per year in tax cuts from the capital gains and dividend changes alone, a savings approximately equal to the median household income of the American family.[6]

funds.[5] Eighty-eight percent of Americans report no capital gains on their tax reports and seventy-five percent of Americans report no dividends. Bush says repeatedly to the voters that his tax cuts return *your* money back to *you*, but the cuts go overwhelmingly to the wealthy. Bush's giant tax cuts, totaling trillions of dollars up to 2010, are the largest handout ever to the rich. Tax specialist Robert Shapiro reports that Bush's 2003 income tax cut "is weighted not to the upper middle class but to the very, very, very rich. In fact, to the top two-tenths of one percent, who receive 15,000 times as much of a tax cut as an average American family."[7] Likewise, a Brookings Institute study shows that Bush's dividend tax cut rewards the wealthy, with those making under $50,000 receiving only 6 percent of the benefits from Bush's tax cut on dividends.[8] Ninety-eight percent of the benefits of Bush's estate tax elimination go to the richest two percent; even Bill Gates,

Sr., has campaigned against eliminating the estate tax, saying it's unfair, and his son doesn't need the money.[9]

The various tax shelter proposals, analyzed in detail by tax specialists Robert Greenstein and Joel Friedman of the Center for Budget and Policy Priorities, allow a wealthy family to shelter from taxation substantial amounts of savings for each "member" each year over the entire lifetime of the owners; that is, once sheltered, no taxes will ever be paid on these funds. Greenstein and Friedman note, "The proposal would confer windfalls of rather massive proportions on the nation's wealthiest individuals."[10]

Under Bush's new savings proposals, a wealthy couple with two children would be able to put $45,000 a year into tax-sheltered saving vehicles on which all earnings would be tax free. (Moreover, this figure does not include amounts the couple could deposit into tax advantaged, employer-based retirement accounts. After 2006, such a couple where both parents are working would be able to put an additional $30,000 a year into such accounts, for a total of $75,000 a year.) Over time, wealthy individuals could shift substantial amounts of their savings and investments into these tax-favored accounts, with the interest, dividends and capital gains income earned on the amounts accruing tax free. The result would be of enormous benefit to wealthy individuals who have large amounts of assets they can shift into these accounts.[11]

ROBERT GREENSTEIN AND JOEL FRIEDMAN,
Center for Budget and Policy Priorities

Closely related to these tax windfalls for the rich is a radical privatization agenda that also transfers resources to big corporations. The proposed legislation for privatizing Social Security will destroy it as a redistributive social contract across generations and turn it into an entrepreneurial scheme for private investment. Despite the turbulence in the markets, privatizing Social Security remains a core goal of Bush's second-term domestic agenda, prioritized in the policy statements of the American Enterprise Institute and Americans for Tax Reform and in other Republican domestic policy statements, and mentioned by Bush in his 2004 State of the Union address. Grover Norquist, President of Americans for Tax Reform, who has the ear of many of Bush's top advisors, highlights Social Security and Medicare privatization as part of a broader agenda to radically downsize government and turn the public sector itself over to the corporations. Norquist says now is the time to "double efforts" to "rein in the spending and regulatory madness . . . Limiting the growth of government will set the infrastructure for all the other center-right victories."[12]

These include the privatization mania that turns public wilderness forests over to the mining and timber companies; water resources over to global conglomerates such as Bechtel; the air waves over to media monopolies such as NewsCorp; educational, health, prison, and social welfare services over to corporations such as Microsoft and General Electric; and even military services over to private military companies such as Dyncorp and Military Professional Resources.

LEAVE *ALL* AMERICANS BEHIND

If I ask you who loses from Econogate, you'll probably say workers and the poor, whose plight under the regime I have chronicled throughout the book. But the more accurate answer is *everyone*. A perfect storm is about not just lies but regime crises, created by the very policies being lied about. Econogate is the cover-up of a looming crisis that is undermining the economy as a whole, despite the appearance of recovery, hurting everyone but the rich in the short term and sabotaging the rich themselves in the long term. The regime is sponsoring policies that suggest an almost suicidal mission as the country rockets toward a fiscal nightmare and toward the kind of devilish structural crisis that fuels and feeds a perfect storm.

Regime change requires exposing what I called in Chapter 1 "the red shift," or runaway deficit. Since the beginning of the current corporate regime in the 1970s, the United States has moved from being a creditor to a debtor nation. Deficits can be good economic medicine in recession, but the current red shift signals America is in unprecedented long-term trouble. Econogate disguises the long-term corporate looting of the national economy that is the most enduring legacy of the current regime. It is undermining the health of the American economic system, leading to the biggest state deficits and the largest service cuts ever seen in U.S. history, threatening the jobs of thousands of public-sector workers and millions in the private sector, while eating away the foundation of investment and economic growth for the long haul.

Regime presidents since Reagan have presided over long-term decline, undermining America's ability to man-

READ IT AND WEEP

In the House-approved Bush budget for FY 2004, cuts would eliminate health coverage for 13.6 million kids, end school lunches for 2.4 million low-income children, end benefits for 65,000 neglected or abused children, and reduce food-stamp benefits from 91 cents to an average of 81 cents a meal.[13]

age the global economy and preserve its own health, even as it seeks to expand military dominance. The current red shift is linked to systemic global overproduction and business's reluctance to invest in and create jobs, as well as the regime's commitment to reducing taxes on the rich while spending big on corporate welfare and the military.

Bush came into office promising fiscal responsibility. Almost as soon as he entered office, he misrepresented the economic viability of his huge 2001 tax cut by claiming that there would be a $5.6 trillion surplus over the next ten years, based on the assumption that there would be no increase in discretionary government spending and no new spending. Such deceptions seem almost comical in light of the vanished surplus. This didn't stop Bush from making similarly deceptive moves to cover his 2003 second round of tax cuts. In the era of massive budget and trade deficits, he said the 2003 cuts would cost $350 billion, but this assumes that a future president and Congress will remove "sunset" provisions and restore many of the taxes that Bush

is cutting, a prospect that almost nobody in Washington believes. If the sunset provisions are not removed, congressional analysts report that the cumulative cost of the Bush
tax cuts will total $1.5 trillion over the next ten years.[14]

> **WHAT THEY SAID:** On February 4, 2003, Bush Budget
> Director Mitch Daniels said, "A federal balanced
> budget remains a high priority for this president."
> **WHAT THEY DID:** A few months later, Bush proposed
> a 2004 budget projecting $475 billion in deficit, even
> larger than the 2003 record-setter, and the Congres-
> sional Budget Office reported that the cumulative
> debt could reach $5.8 trillion by 2013.[15]

In what should become one of the most infamous of
Bush's deceptions, he suppressed his own Treasury Department's study projecting a succession of long-term future deficits, based on current government obligations
amounting to an astonishing *$44 trillion*.[16] Bush chose to
keep this study out of his 2004 budget, not surprising since
the report said it would take virtual abolition of federal
discretionary social spending or a whopping 66 percent
across-the-board income tax increase to solve the problem.[17] A Goldman Sachs study from about the same time
projects deficits over the next decade amounting to $4.5
trillion, comparable to the estimate by the Congressional
Budget Office cited above, causing more than a two-thirds
increase in the national debt. That debt will keep rising
because of the explosive increase in the aging population,
higher price tags on Social Security and Medicare, and
mushrooming military costs.[18]

Princeton economist and *New York Times* columnist
Paul Krugman has discussed the implications of the explo-

sively growing debts in stark terms. "There is now a huge structural gap—that is, a gap that won't go away even if the economy recovers—between U.S. spending and revenue. For the time being, borrowing can fill that gap. But eventually there must be either a large tax increase or major cuts in popular programs."[19]

Astronomical debt, fueled by the regime's giant tax cuts and big military spending, is a regime plan to "starve the beast," that is, to use the huge deficits to force cuts in social spending. But that approach is unlikely to solve the problem, partly because the public won't accept the trashing of Social Security and Medicare, and Congress will keep spending on corporate welfare as well as the social kind. Eventually, the deficits will cause deeper problems, undermining the conditions of growth.

Rising interest rates, plunging savings, and growing dependency on foreign investors undermine conditions for long-term growth and stability, doing damage not only to workers cut off from jobs and social welfare, but also to the very corporations causing the problems by feeding on ballooning corporate welfare.

It gets worse. Think about the growing trade deficit, a second mushrooming debt that Nobel Prize–winning economists Franco Modigliani and Robert Solow call "the greatest potential danger facing the economy in the years to come."[20] As economic analyst Jeff Faux points out, this form of debt "is now 22% of GDP. Assuming a recovery, the U.S. economy is on a trajectory to a [trade deficit] debt burden of roughly 40% of GDP within five years." The regime's fiscal and trade policies contributed to these scary deficits by facilitating the drastic flight of manufacturing jobs and making it difficult to close the trade gap through expanding exports.[21]

A different regime—willing to tax the rich, reduce military spending, and invest in the people—could alter this drastic course. But such a policy would go against the short-term greed of regime elites. The implications for the regime and the nation are frightening. This regime is so extreme that it is spending itself to death, a marvelous irony since it's allegedly committed to small government and fiscal responsibility. Such extremism is the regime's own gift to you—if you want regime change—since, as I show in the next chapter, it commits regime leaders to a form of systemic suicide.

The crisis won't come immediately . . . But at a certain point we'll have a Wile E. Coyote moment. For those not familiar with the Road Runner cartoons, Mr. Coyote had a habit of running off cliffs and taking several steps on thin air before noticing that there was nothing underneath his feet. Only then would he plunge.

What will that plunge look like? It will certainly involve a sharp fall in the dollar and a sharp rise in interest rates. In the worst-case scenario, the government's access to borrowing will be cut off, creating a cash crisis that throws the nation into chaos.[22]

PAUL KRUGMAN, The New York Times

Liberty . . . means allowing people freely to say things
you do not want to hear. GEORGE ORWELL

CHAPTER 8

THE RULES OF EXTREMISM

I went to jail briefly for civil disobedience in support of a "janitors for justice" protest event in Boston in 2002. It was a different and more frightening experience than my other experiences with the prison system, which were during 1960s antiwar protests before the current regime. This time, all those committing civil disobedience were arrested, fingerprinted, booked, and eventually sent to individual cells. I noticed on the walls of the police station dozens of postings from Washington about terrorism. After we were booked and sent to cells, the police told us that our detention was indefinite, pending word from Washington regarding whether we were suspects for terrorism. They sent our fingerprints and records to Washington to determine whether any of us might be under surveillance by the CIA or FBI. Sitting isolated in a cell, unaware of how long I would be detained and feeling that I might be deprived of my right to talk to lawyers and get help, was quite different than contemplating the Patriot Act from my office. For anyone who doubts whether civil liberties and the Bill of Rights matter, I recommend an involuntary stay in a jail cell under the new conditions.

U.S. regimes have historically conformed to two basic rules. One is the "constitutional rule": that they pledge allegiance to constitutional democracy, specifically the procedural guarantees of free elections, civil liberties, and the Bill of Rights. The second, the "capitalist rule," is that they preserve a sustainable capitalism as the nation's economic order.

The Bush administration is extremist on both counts. My jail experience may have oversensitized me, but the only threats to civil liberties as dire as the Patriot Act and other antiterrorism measures was during the Wilson administration toward the end of World War I, and the early Eisenhower years when McCarthyism ran wild. As for economic extremism, Bush might be remembered as the president who created so much red ink and so few jobs that he endangered capitalism itself. Even if Bush wins in 2004, this extremism will ultimately lead to the death of the regime.

Bush's extremism is rooted in the broader regime. When Barry Goldwater said in 1964, "Extremism in the pursuit of liberty is no vice," he was signaling the spirit of the coming regime. The New Right and the neoconservatives of the 1970s were bold thinkers seen as extremists in their time. But their extremism was a strength then, since it takes radicalism to mobilize the masses and change regimes, and they were not yet in a position of power that would allow the public to absorb how far beyond the two cardinal rules they would take the country.

The extremism of the current regime has fluctuated between its four presidents. Reagan and Bush, Jr., are the most extreme faces of the regime, with Bush more the political son of Reagan than of his father. Bush, Sr., and Clinton were less extreme, even though both used repressive measures in the name of national security to restrict domestic dissent, and both rejected the New Deal, embracing economic policies that helped destabilize financial markets and global capitalism.

Identifying extremism is difficult because regimes change the political conversation and make their own vision mainstream. During the New Deal regime, liberalism was mainstream. Under the current regime, it has become the "L word," almost a form of extremism in itself. This is a sign of how powerfully regimes transform the terms of discourse, and it shows that extremism has an element of "relativity" about it.

Nonetheless, the two rules offer reliable historical guidelines that define extremism in the United States since the Civil War. My aim in this chapter is to show how the most extreme president of an extremist regime has breached both rules, opening up new prospects for regime change. I focus here on the Bush administration, but the trends I describe clearly reflect regime policies begun under Reagan. A regime begun as extremist will ultimately succumb to regime change because of its own extremism.

WHAT HAPPENED TO MY CIVIL LIBERTIES?

The Bush threat to the constitutional rule begins with civil liberties and the Patriot Act. The Patriot Act is a modern version of the espionage acts of 1917 and 1918 passed by the Wilson administration during World War I.[1] Among other things, the Patriot Act allows the federal government to tap your phone, read your snail mail and email, get access to your financial and medical records, find out what books you checked out from the library, snoop on activist groups you might join, and detain you in jail indefinitely without formal charges.

You think they wouldn't do it to you, but don't be so sure. When I was in jail, they insisted I would be held until they had cleared in Washington that I wasn't on Osama's payroll. The same was true for the other staid and proper professors, union leaders, church leaders, and even a local city councilor who had gone to bat for the janitors. Anyone can be considered a terrorist suspect, which is why many constitutional lawyers view the Patriot Act as a historic erosion of the Bill of Rights not just for terrorists but for all Americans. On November 9, 2003, Al Gore publicly called for the repeal of the Patriot Act, arguing that it involves "mass violations of civil liberties."[2]

The threat to civil liberties in the Patriot Act and the "son of Patriot," a successor domestic security measure being discussed, are part of a much broader assault on constitutional rights, fired up under Reagan in the name of the war on the "Evil Empire" and now as part of the war on terrorism. Since "homeland security" is based on intelligence and surveillance, and the threats from bioweapons or a

> *They that can give up essential liberty to obtain a little temporary safety deserve neither liberty nor safety.*
>
> BENJAMIN FRANKLIN, 1759

single nuclear weapon in the hands of a terrorist are so frightening, the war on terrorism offers a perfect umbrella for a regime seeking to redefine historical understandings of constitutional democracy. It provides the rationale for the secrecy, tight control of information and dissent, and reinterpretation of traditional constitutional rights that were the trademark of the regime even prior to 9/11.

HOW MANY FLORIDAS DOES IT TAKE TO ELECT A PRESIDENT?

Beyond respect for civil liberties, the constitutional rule requires respect for procedural democracy: fair and free elections and rule of law. Now many Americans felt this had been solved after slaves were freed, the poll tax ended, and women got the right to vote. In this regime, you'd better think again.

The integrity of procedural democracy became a crisis in Bush's election to office, when a mountain of procedural violations in Florida contributed to Bush's election. Remember how Florida helped us see what "free elections" really means?

The famous butterfly and punch card hanging chad ballots

The unorthodox interpretation of the Fourteenth Amendment, by the 5 to 4 majority of the U.S. Supreme Court, that put Bush in the White House

The reports of voters, mainly minorities, turned away
from the polls

The Jeb Bush administration's illegal decision in Florida
to disenfranchise voters who had committed misdemeanors or felonies in either Florida or other states
(Note: Florida law permits denying the vote to con-
victed felons in Florida, disenfranchising thousands
of voters, but it does not allow denying voting rights
to those who committed misdemeanors or felonies
in other states, served their time, and subsequently
moved to Florida.)

Greg Palast and other investigative reporters have documented that thousands of voters were illegally scrubbed
from the voting rolls in Florida, the majority of them minorities who vote Democratic, and that they could have
swung the election.[3] Palast and the others do not *prove* that
George W. Bush approved these registration violations regarding felons, minorities, etc., but the fact that they were
carried out under his brother, Governor Jeb Bush, and
were not investigated by the federal government after being exposed, is itself a serious indictment. From 2000 to
2003, 38 percent of the American electorate has consis-
tently told pollsters that they regard Bush's election as ille-
gitimate because of the Florida debacle, an astonishing loss
of faith in the most fundamental rules of the game.

Since these "deviations" in procedural democracy in
Florida, the people's faith in the electoral process has been
subjected to continuing assaults in states all over the country. To name a few:

Texas: What a scene! Texan Democratic legislators all
jumped on a bus and drove out of state to deny the

Republicans the ability to push through a radical and unfair redistricting scheme. They had to eventually come back, but they alerted Americans to a new danger: the rush to manipulate and gerrymander districts that is sweeping state legislatures across the country. In Florida, Michigan, Ohio, and Pennsylvania, Republican legislators recarved districts into weird shapes such as "upside-down Chinese dragons," ensuring that Republicans can easily win fifty-one of the seventy-seven congressional seats in these states, whose populations are evenly divided between the two parties.[4]

California: When I was in Europe in October 2003, the first and only thing people wanted to talk about was Arnold Schwarzenegger. Was the Terminator terminating free elections as we know them? The 2003 gubernatorial recall circus in California, a move to oust a sitting governor through extraprocedural means that led to Arnold Schwarzenegger's election, created a mini-crisis in constitutional procedures that captured international attention. Many doubted that enough time was available to buy and set up modern voting machines, as well as publicize and vet the ballot of 136 candidates as required by law, to ensure that all votes would be registered accurately. But hey, after Florida, we were getting used to it.

Washington, D.C.: While the Bush administration is not responsible for all these procedural democratic deficits, it has failed to fund adequately the reform and funding of the electoral processes proposed in the Help America Vote Act, passed by Congress in 2002. One such failure—to fund computerized voting equipment—might actually turn out to be a surprising stroke of luck; see "Voter Beware."

VOTER BEWARE

Electronic, or optical scanning, voting machines need more funding to ensure protection against fraud, since there is no paper record to check. Until then, paper ballots —with or without chads—are better. By the way, Walden O'Dell, the CEO of Diebold, Inc., one of the largest manufacturers of computerized voting machines, is a major GOP fund-raiser. O'Dell has stated that he is committed to "helping Ohio deliver its electoral votes" to President Bush.[5]

Bush has failed to follow through on the Help America Vote provisions for voter education, voter access, and registration reforms that might move us back toward free and fair elections. Moreover, under Karl Rove the national Republican Party has taken the lead to ensure that redistricting, disenfranchisement of felons, campaign finance reform, and other measures tilt the electoral processes to favor Bush's reelection and a Republican Congress. The Bush administration has also resisted efforts to make registering and voting easier through such measures as changing elections to weekends, declaring Election Day a national holiday, allowing election-day registration, or having people automatically registered when they get a driver's license.

GET THE WORD OUT ABOUT
"FREE ELECTIONS"

The violation of the constitutional rule by an extreme regime sets up the condition for a regime change that might otherwise be substantially delayed. The challenge in regime change politics in 2004 and beyond is to demonstrate to Americans of all political persuasions that the constitutional rule has been violated, and that Bush is a major part of the problem. It is largely a matter of public education to help the majority of Americans recognize the gravity of what they already believe: U.S. elections are no longer free, fair, or credible.

For the past several decades, former President Jimmy Carter has been going around the world to monitor and certify the fairness of elections in poor nations such as El Salvador. It is time for Carter to come home. He should play the same observer role in the United States that he has abroad, making clear to U.S. voters how to determine whether their own elections are fair and helping citizens certify them. Civic groups, whether the League of Women Voters or Common Cause or Nader's Public Interest Research Groups (PIRGs), should aggressively pursue such a public campaign during the entire 2004 elections and beyond, engaging in their own certification programs. Awakening the public to systemic electoral fraud, the weakening of the Bill of Rights, and the crisis of procedural democracy is a surefire, essential way to get real about the current regime and hasten the looming regime change we need.

TRULY FREE
ELECTIONS

It's time to make "free elections" free. Here are a few steps that would help.

> Promote much wider public education about what happened in Florida.
>
> Constitutional lawyers should spell out the Orwellian implications of the Bush war on terrorism in op-ed pages across the country, making sure that the Patriot Act is understood by every voter going into the polls.
>
> During the electoral season and afterward, every major newspaper and television network across the country should run investigative campaigns on the funding and monitoring of elections; election machines; registration and balloting procedures; the redistricting process; the exclusion of millions of prisoners, ex-convicts, and other citizens from voting rights; and the comparison of U.S. registration and voting procedures to those in other nations.
>
> All high school civics teachers should require their students to investigate these issues. Excellent books and articles to get them started have already been published.[6]

CORPORATIONS AGAINST
CAPITALISM: EXTREME ECONOMICS

MEET PETER SORLEY

Peter, forty-three years old, has a degree from The College of the Holy Cross and is an aspiring writer. He has worked in several full-time jobs, including for a furniture company, a deli, and the post office. He has also written a novel, driven a cab, and worked as a temp. But right now, he says, his career is being a "medical whore."

"I've done a lot of medical tests during the last nine months," he starts out when I inquire about his job. "Medical tests?" I ask. "Well, there is a place nearby where they test Ibuprofen and you go in for about four or five days and they take blood samples. They want to see how fast it metabolizes, and you pick up a couple hundred bucks that way."

Peter says, "When you do the medical tests, your expenses are only telephone and rent. Everything else is taken care of." He says he can do better on this job than in many low-wage full-time jobs. "You take home at least four hundred twenty-five a week. It's a career to a point, until you realize it's not your chosen profession."

I tell Peter this seems like an extreme career and wonder how he ended up there. He says he hates temping but often doesn't have a choice. "I don't care to live that kind of existence, period. It's too damn straining to go into this temp job, with a floor full of people, trying to relate to them and then realizing, 'Holy mackerel! In six weeks, I'm not going to be around here.' And it doesn't mean I didn't *want to be there; it's just too damn stressful and awkward to have to associate, disassociate, associate, disassociate."*

Peter says the interpersonal stress is overwhelming. "You're meeting a stranger, you need to get together to get the work done, and being the temp, deep down inside, whether it's conscious or not, you know it's temporary and it screws up your digestive system." To avoid the stress in one temp clerical job, "every day I took my lunch in the garage."

The second rule of U.S. regimes is to preserve capitalism. The extreme regime is historically one that threatens to undermine "free markets" or otherwise challenge a market economy. The Populists in the 1890s went down to defeat partly because they were correctly seen as challenging corporate capitalism and were thus branded the harbingers of an extreme regime. This has also plagued the efforts of Left and progressive groups explicitly seeking to replace capitalism with socialism or other egalitarian alternatives. Recall that an extreme regime is not necessarily wrong in principle, but it is so out of step with U.S. historical convention that it is difficult to create or sustain.

Peter Sorley is not just a hard-luck worker, any more than the others profiled in this book. His "extreme career" reflects the extremism of the regime. Peter's loss of a viable career mirrors the erosion of a sustainable economy, the inevitable outcome of this regime's economic approach.

The notion that the current regime is violating the capitalist rule seems unbelievable on its face, since I have made clear that it is a corporate regime dedicated to profit and corporate interests. Yet the current regime, and particularly the Bush administration, is endangering the viability of the global capitalist order and has already introduced an extreme statist, debt-ridden economy at home incompatible with historical capitalist concepts. This leads to the possibility that corporations themselves, despite their current marriage to the Bush administration, could eventually seek to depose the regime. It also leads to the prospect that millions more will join Peter in the ranks of the economically dispossessed, unable to find full-time, permanent, or well-paying jobs. Peter has no money to spend on anything but "rent, food, and telephone," and he is in serious debt. As millions more are thrown into the same circumstances, sustainable capitalism is being undermined.

THE ANTI-CAPITALIST CORPORATE REGIME

A corporate regime is not the same thing as a capitalist or market system. A corporate regime puts corporate monopoly above the competition of markets, corporate power above that of the citizens, and profits above people. Unlike traditional nineteenth-century capitalist orders rooted in local competitive businesses, today's global corporate system is a huge managed system, directed by the corporate state in alliance with monopolistic global companies. The regime rules in the name of the free market, but it has actually become a statist system, dependent on state intervention for the management of the overall economy, and for regulation and control of competition. The state finances education, research, and infrastructure that corporations need, and corporations are increasingly dependent on subsidies for global competitiveness.[7]

Although the statist character of corporate regimes began to emerge a century ago, it has assumed a qualitatively different character. The vast size of the state, its intimate management of every sector of the economy, and the increasing dependency of corporations on corporate welfare make a mockery of free-market rhetoric, while creating a genuine transformation in the nature of the economic system. In Europe, the melding of corporation and state led in the 1930s to "national socialism," or fascism, in Germany and Italy. The corporate/state merger in America today is unique, and it might better be called simply *corpocracy* (as explained in Chapter 1), one of the main pillars upholding the current regime. However named, it departs radically from the historic concept of the "private" economy in a "free market" capitalism.[8]

This immediately leads to the question of how such a regime, in which the state is devoted to corporate rather than public interest, can violate the capitalist rule by undermining the viability of both the U.S. and the global economy. This partly reflects contradictions, discussed in Chapter 7, leading to huge, unsustainable debt and decline. But it is more immediately related to two closely related attributes of the current regime: its short-term thinking and its abandonment of elite stewardship.

SHORT-TERMISM

Are you a day trader? Do you move money in and out of stocks for the quick kill? Well, whether you do or not, it's now the way of the world—or at least of this regime. About two trillion dollars swirl around the world each day looking for the highest return on corporate issues, currency bets, pork bellies, or day trades. The regime has become a giant planetary casino. Yippee!

Short-term thinking is endemic to the current regime, rooted structurally in the way its financial markets are organized. Since the late 1970s, when financial services in the United States began to be deregulated at home and "liberalized" in the world economy, the financial markets have operated on an increasingly short-term principle, seeking the highest short-term profit. Money chases the shortest-term return from purely financial transactions, whether they are currency trading, commodity trading, or derivatives betting. Whole industries shift toward the short-term financial model, exemplified by Enron, which helped transform the global energy business from energy production to trading of energy futures.[9]

Such financialization—a shift toward an economy organized around short-term, often speculative, financial flows—has historically been associated with systemic economic decline. Sociologist and world system theorist Giovanni Arrighi argues that financialization is the critical historical indicator of hegemonic economic crisis. For example, it led to the craze in tulip speculation during the decline of the Dutch empire, a possible equivalent to the NASDAQ high-tech speculative boom and bust of the late 1990s.[10]

In the United States today, financialization is contributing to private and state indebtedness on a grand scale. And as Paul Krugman argues, the Bush regime, by running unprecedented deficits in the service of short-term tax cuts for the rich, is engaged in a "great unraveling," which could ultimately bring down the corporate system itself.[11]

Financialization and short-term thinking are closely associated with a second attribute of the current regime, also economically ruinous and in violation of the capitalist rule: the abandonment of elite stewardship. It involves the rise of a corporate elite that abandons the responsibility of maintaining the viability of the system over time. The elite resorts to getting as much money as it can now, before it ejects the golden parachute for itself.

The Enron scandal exposed the realities. Consider the money pulled down between 1999 and 2001 by the CEOs of three of the major firms involved.[12]

TYCO CEO L. D. Kozlowski made $332,765,196.
Q-West CEO J. P. Nacchio earned $266,332,104.
Enron CEO K. L. Lay raked in $250,834,250.

Yes, that's right, three hundred and thirty-two million dollars for Kozlowski! All twenty-three companies under investigation for accounting scandals bring up even more shocking figures.

The twenty-three CEOs earned an average of $62 million from 1999 to 2001, compared with an average of $36 million for all CEOs in the annual *Business Week* executive pay survey.

Collectively, the CEOs at firms under investigation pocketed $1.4 billion from 1999 to 2001. While these executives are cushioned by the vast wealth they have accumulated, their shareholders and employees are dealing with massive losses. Between January 1, 2000, and July 21, 2002, the value of shares at these firms plunged by $530 billion, about 73 percent of their total value.[13]

The pattern of executives bringing down the company to make hundreds of millions in a hurry doesn't apply just to the Enron affair. The same thing happened during the meltdown of the NASDAQ and Dow in the late 1990s. As *Fortune* magazine put it,

> The dirty little secret of the crash is that even as investors were losing 70 percent, 90 percent, even in some cases all of their holdings, top officials of many of the companies that have crashed the hardest were getting immensely, extraordinarily, obscenely wealthy.[14]

Analysts view this as a product of greed typical of corporate regimes, notably in the Gilded Age. But while nobody can dispute the astonishing greed of the current corporate elites, immortalized in the film *Wall Street,* the greed in the current regime is different than in the Gilded Age. In that era, the robber barons were ferociously greedy but simultaneously worked to build the productive economy and sustain it for the long haul. Today, the greed of regime elites is contributing to systemic decline. Nobody is left to watch out for the long-term interests of the system.

The decline of elite stewardship—and the rise of self-dealing elites who are cashing in on the Enron, Putnam, and other great corporate scandals of the day—has its roots in structural conditions related to what sociologist Michael Useem calls "investor capitalism."[15] This is the shift toward a corporate order driven by the short-term requirements of Wall Street. The money managers of the big institutional investors, such as Fidelity or Vanguard or the big pension funds, run the show, focusing on quarterly profits and leaving executives little room for long-term strategic thinking. The executives are well rewarded for their capitulation,

in the form of their own multimillion-dollar compensation packages and the golden parachutes that await them as they move from one company to the next.[16]

Regime change politics should be an indictment of a regime elite that has abandoned its own project. In the 1980s, in films like *Wall Street* and *Other People's Money,* Hollywood took on the unexpected role of populist educator, going after the fat cats who buy companies only to chop them up and sell them for parts. Today, the cutting edge of such popular education in Hollywood has been taken up by independent filmmakers such as Michael Moore, who in his Oscar–winning film, *Bowling for Columbine,* and his books, *Stupid White Men* and *Dude, Where's My Country?,* continued the exposé of corporations that he began with *Roger and Me.* Enron, WorldCom, Putnam, and all the other bankrupt perpetrators of financial fraud are, by their own blatant self-dealing, educating the public about how they are enriching themselves at everyone else's expense. What Moore doesn't make clear enough is that these elites are captains on the *Titanic*, not only endangering the rest of the population but also steering the ship into a gigantic iceberg destined to sink its own corporate enterprises.

This aspect of regime change politics has a distinctly Zen flavor. Teaching that the corporate regime violates the capitalist rule offers the virtue of counterintuitive surprise, at odds with traditional notions of dissent against the system. Regime change is necessary not just to save the rest of us, but to save capitalism, much as the New Deal regime did. Capitalism has always bred greed. But extreme greed, modeled so nakedly in this regime, will bring down capitalism itself.

PART III

Regime Change

*M*ost political books attack a problem but offer no solutions, leaving the reader feeling helpless and ready to reach for some Prozac. To avoid that, I have written an extended final section to show that there is hope for regime change, and to explain how we might achieve it.

Many Americans are disenchanted with the current regime but don't see any realistic alternatives. The idea that there is no alternative is a self-fulfilling prophecy. We can create regime change only when we believe that an alternative exists.

The great task of the twenty-first century is to determine what a postcorporate regime will look like. What is an America freed from corporate rule? We are so accustomed to the reign of big corporations that we scarcely bother to ask the question.

Here, I try to ask *and* to answer it. I offer a vision that lies within our grasp of the next regime. While some will find my agenda idealistic, it seems so only because it is not achievable within the current regime. Regimes are systems for limiting the imagination and locking us into the current terms of discourse. When a regime falls, as it did in 1932 and in 1980, changes that looked impossible can become common sense.

New crises are already fanning the flames of social movements seeking regime change. Regime change happens because of terminal socioeconomic crises such as I have just described in Part II, and the rise of social movements from among the burning people sucked into the regime volcano. In Part III, I show that these movements are already on the scene and argue that, despite their lack of big money, they are worthy challengers of the corporate goliaths.

I then turn in detail to the regime that these movements are fighting for. While radical in many ways, it represents a return to the basic principles of democracy on which the country was founded. The next regime will be fundamentally conservative, since it will reestablish the country on the principles of popular sovereignty and accountable government enshrined in the Constitution.

Because the agenda goes back to the values of the Founders, it can attract Americans from across the political spectrum. In the final chapter, I show that regime change depends on a major political realignment that creates a new "big tent."

Einstein said, "The world is a dangerous place not because of those who do evil, but [because of] those who look on and do nothing." Today, this is a call for Americans who are not happy with their government to fight for regime change at home. I suggest here that you can pitch in and make a difference.

CHAPTER 9

REGIME CHANGE BEGINS WITH YOU

It is a struggle between the robbers and the robbed.[1]

SOCKLESS JERRY SIMPSON,
Populist activist, 1890s

Without question we need regime change at home, and it all depends on you. All through U.S. history, corporate regimes have changed entirely because of ordinary citizens just like yourself. If you believe regime change is necessary and, along with your fellow citizens, decide that you're going to do something about it, it will happen. And it will be one of the most important and rewarding things you do in your whole life.

Of course, it is hardly surprising that it is up to you. Remember, the whole reason for regime change is that ordinary citizens like you have lost control—in overstressed workplaces, underfunded communities, and unrepresentative governments. The people who run this regime—the fat cats in the corporations and their pals in the White House and Congress—will fight regime change until the end, even as terminal crises weaken their hold. Yes, the regime crises described in Part II are a hellish witch's brew that will eventually bring down the regime. But it takes powerful movements of people like you and me to finish the job. Such movements are revving up, and I show in this chapter that you should help them make history and send the regime packing.

You're probably thinking that a person like yourself can't fight City Hall, let alone the biggest corporations in the world. But when you link up with many more like yourself, the equation begins to change. When citizens act together in what I call the Active Citizens' Network (see Chapter 10 for more details), the corporate regime will lose power and eventually be defeated. And the corporations know it. After the 1999 Battle of Seattle, when just fifty thousand Americans went out on the streets to protest corporate globalization, corporate leaders went into a panic trying to figure out why people were so angry and what they could do to settle them down.

Every change of a corporate regime in U.S. history has been tied to a dramatic growth in popular citizen activity and movements, such as the nineteenth-century Populists or the New Deal unions. The explosion of social movements in the endgame of regimes reflects the rise of terminal crises. Regimes fall because they can no longer patch up crises that intensify the stress and suffering of citizens like you. In the endgame, people stop trusting the elites, get mad as hell, and decide to take matters into their own hands.

Now you may be thinking that you're not an activist. But the Active Citizens' Network is bigger than protest groups. You're almost certainly part of it now, in your church, neighborhood association, union, or civic group. If you've ever emailed a friend an op-ed piece or even talked with fellow workers or neighbors about some of the issues discussed in this book, you're an active citizen and part of the network. In fact, just by reading this book you're engaging in active citizenship that can help create regime change.

When you do any of these things, you contribute to a process, already under way with the rise of grassroots citizens' movements—including unions, antiwar networks, antiglobalization activists, and religious communities—that seek to change public consciousness and create a different regime. These citizens' or social movements are the catalyzers of regime change: they have created regime change in the past and they are starting to do so again.

Keep three things in mind. First, the movements are ultimately based in the civic associations of people like you. Americans have always been individualists, but also civic "associators" who know how to get together and help run their own communities—that's how Alexis de Tocqueville described us one hundred and fifty years ago to his fellow Europeans. And as Howard Zinn has shown in his wonderful *People's History of the United States,* we have also always been a nation of strong grassroots movements—from the abolitionists to the suffragists—who have made America the great country it is!

Second, even regime-busting protest movements are always a small percentage of the population. But they speak for a much larger number of people who lack the time or temperament to get out in the streets. The abolitionists helped bring down slavery, but they were just a fraction of the populace, as were both the Populists and Progressives a century ago.

Third, the citizens' movements cannot create regime change without transforming the political parties—either by taking over one of the mainstream parties or by creating third parties. In the last two sections of this chapter, I look briefly at the role of the Democratic Party, as well as third parties like the Greens.

IT'S UP TO YOU AND ME

While I pay a lot of attention to the Democratic Party all through this book, always remember this: regime change has to come from you and me. The Democratic Party calls itself the party of the people, but it isn't. We will have to drag it away from its comfortable perch in corporate America and force it to act as well as speak in our name. If it won't, we will create a new party, as the Gilded Age Populists did!

REMEMBER THE POPULISTS!

If you don't think you and your fellow Americans are capable of all this, just recall the Populist movements of a century ago. By the mid 1880s, Rockefeller, J. P. Morgan, Andrew Carnegie, and other robber barons had consolidated their control over Washington, elected a long string of Republican corporate puppet presidents, and turned themselves into billionaires. But farmers and workers found themselves facing crises of survival. Social movements began coalescing in the early 1890s to overthrow the first corporate regime. The Populists were the most important, made up mainly of heartland farmers deep in debt. The leading historian of the Populists, Lawrence Goodwyn, calls them "the flowering of the largest democratic mass movement in American history."[2]

The Populist agenda was to return control of the country from the thieving corporations to the people. Kansan Populist Mary Lease said, *"We're going to raise less corn and more hell."* She declared, "Wall Street owns the country. It is no longer a government of the people, by the people, and for the people, but a government of Wall Street, by Wall Street, and for Wall Street."[3]

The solution: "The corporation has absorbed the community. The community must now absorb the corporation."[4] For the Populists this meant abolishing the private banking system, breaking up Rockefeller's trusts and Morgan's financial empire, getting big money out of Washington, and rebuilding the economy around new producer cooperatives.

The Populists sought "legislation as shall secure to our

people freedom from the onerous and shameful abuses that the industrial classes are now suffering at the hands of capitalists and powerful corporations."[5] They challenged corporate social Darwinism with a political philosophy of cooperativism and Jeffersonian democracy. The Populists created their own farmers' co-ops, instituting cooperative purchasing and marketing and envisioning a whole economy based on cooperative principles.[6]

In 1892, they founded a third party, the People's Party, and ran a credible race on a platform of economic democracy. Focusing on corporate power and greed, they realized they would be "confronted by a vast and splendidly equipped army of extortionists, usurers, and oppressors." But they refused to be cowed, proclaiming, "We are at the dawn of the golden age of popular power."[7] In 1896, they captured the Democratic Party and ran their own leader, William Jennings Bryan, as the Democratic candidate for president. Populism emerged as the classic American form of opposition to corporate regimes, and while the Populist movement was defeated by the big money of the robber barons and its own internal failures to speak to immigrant workers, it helped give rise to the regime change of Teddy Roosevelt's Progressives, who preserved capitalism but reformed the corporate order and helped "bust the trusts."

THE NEW POPULISTS

At the Battle of Seattle, the 1999 surprising explosion at the World Trade Organization (WTO) meeting of the antiglobalization movement in the United States, I walked through the tear-gassed streets with a cell phone. Every block or so, I got a call from another radio or newspaper reporter with more questions. One talk-show host even caught me at dinner and wouldn't let me finish my meal until I answered his questions.

A new populism is rising. Today, grassroots movements are sprouting, a sign of the coming battle for regime change. While still largely under the radar screen of the mass media, we are entering an era of on-the-ground and on-the-net grassroots political activism. Beyond the anti-globalization activists who pop up at every meeting of the world's financial elites, the most visible activists were the millions of people all over the world who spontaneously took to the streets in 2002 and 2003 to protest Bush's invasion of Iraq, creating the largest peace movement in history. These included millions of Americans, many in the mainstream, who had never demonstrated before, and who remain deeply distressed about the U.S. presence in Iraq. They were the ones who began waving colorful posters reading "Regime Change Begins at Home."

The 1999 Seattle gathering of "turtles and teamsters"—environmentalists and workers who had never been on the block together—symbolized the first big coming together of social movements unifying against this corporate regime. It was quite an experience. I talked with burly teamsters marching alongside eco-activists and college students with nose rings, while grandparents pushed kids in strollers. America was coming together in an unprecedented way.

Movements of ordinary citizens—like you and me—are destined to grow rapidly as the regime begins to crack under the weight of its own crises and contradictions. Four elements of the growing regime-busting movements will carry us to success:

> We are riding the wave of the Internet.
> We are acting globally as well as locally.
> We are blooming on campuses.
> We are multicultural and multicoalitional.

CITIZENS' MOVEMENTS.ORG

Regime change is possible because these movements are on the cusp of a massive growth in their capacity to reach and awaken the general public. One reason is the revolution in grassroots politics that the Internet makes possible. During the Iraq war, a group called MoveOn, known to most activists as MoveOn.org, helped transform the political world. Formed by two young people, it emerged as an online network coordinating activism among hundreds of thousands of antiwar citizens. Before the war, MoveOn helped shape global campaigns that deluged congressional offices daily with hundreds of thousands of emails, almost making it impossible for Washington to function.

MoveOn is one amazing organization! It has changed the way politics as usual works in America, proving that the Internet allows movements without much money or visibility to come together and make a vast impact on the public conversation. Along with at least a million other Americans on its listserv, I get emails from MoveOn every week, educating me about current initiatives and allowing me to communicate my views on vital issues to Congress or the White House with a simple click of my mouse. MoveOn has staying power, continuing to function months after the war and to wage battles about corporate power in Iraq and Washington. When the Federal Communications Commission (FCC) deregulated the mass media in 2003, allowing a few giant companies such as Fox, Disney, and AOL–Time Warner to own multiple radio, TV, and newspaper outlets in any given city, MoveOn sent emails to its listserv, encouraging people to call their congressional representatives to tell them to repeal the FCC rules. Thousands made the calls, and Congress launched a major effort to rescind the procorporate FCC decisions, leading the Senate to vote to block the FCC ruling.

MoveOn.org is just one of thousands of online activist networks mobilizing the new Populists around everything from campaign finance to globalization to children's rights. Whichever issue you care about, I guarantee you can find an online network or listserv that can get you educated and connected. As I was writing this, I got an email from somebody just letting me know of a few websites that he thought all his friends should know about—just a tiny smattering of the thousands out there: www.MoveOn.org, www.Act4victory.org, and www.Truemajority.org.

Thousands of movement websites are geared toward specific groups of citizens. Other websites are for wider coalitions of groups, and so many thousands of them exist that directories have popped up on the web just to help you find them. A website called Social Justice Connections describes some colorfully (see "Online Networks of Networks").

Increasingly, social movements are networks mirroring the structure of the Internet itself and taking the form of new kinds of political actors like MoveOn. They are fluid,

ONLINE NETWORKS OF NETWORKS

Social Justice Connections is a great source for anybody who wants to get involved in U.S. regime change. This list is taken from its website at http://www.shentel.net/sjc/links4.html; check out the Appendix for more.[8]

CTCNet unites grassroots community technology centers around the nation. High tech at the grass roots.

The Institute for Global Communications, whose component networks include **PeaceNet, EcoNet, ConflictNet, LaborNet,** and **WomensNet,** provides links to a wide range of progressive organizations, as well as information on its own services.

Macrocosm USA is an ambitious effort to list peace, environmental, health, and justice resources in a searchable database.

National Organizers Alliance connects progressive organizers and strengthens our ability to do organizing well. Fun is also emphasized.

NativeWeb is a well-organized and attractive place to start looking for connections to indigenous peoples, especially from North and South America.

WebActive offers not only a directory, but also current information on progressive activities.

Women's Action for New Directions does exciting and practical grassroots work for peace and empowerment.

multi-issue, and coalition-oriented, bringing together hundreds, thousands, or millions of people in evolving and spontaneous protests and policy initiatives. Far different from a political party, they nonetheless represent an increasingly effective way for ordinary people without much money to help shape political conversations in the country and the world.

One local example I admire is the Boston Global Action Network (BGAN), a coalition of labor, immigrant, student, and community groups. The organizations focus on their own special issues but come together to support each other's initiatives. In the Boston area, they have launched many anticorporate initiatives on immigrant rights, the living wage, social service cuts, and corporate outsourcing that affect all the organizations in the network, helping people make the link between local labor and social crises and the global economy. BGAN is also networked with similar coalitions in other cities and countries, one small part of a global justice network made up of thousands of smaller local networks.[9]

PLANETARY MOVEMENTS

This brings us to another completely new strength of today's regime change movements. Activists are linking up with citizens in other countries to create regime change in many nations simultaneously and in the global corporate order itself.

In the fall of 2003, I did a book tour in Germany and Austria sponsored by a European movement called ATTAC. ATTAC is a remarkable group of international activists in forty-seven different countries. They have a common interest in global justice issues, but the ATTAC in each country has its own agenda. While it is a global movement, its strength is the vibrancy of its chapters, which mobilize people in their local communities around populist issues. When I spoke in Munich, Germany, the local ATTAC had just successfully organized to prevent a global company from taking over the local public subway system. ATTAC groups come together in places like the Global Social Forum, a worldwide convention of social movements and nongovernmental organizations (NGOs) to chart out a new system of globalization.

Historically, populist national movements operated in isolation from those in other countries. Today, movements all over the world are reconstituting themselves as part of a giant anticorporate, prodemocracy planetary coalition never seen before. Sweatshop activists in Boston are emailing daily with sweatshop workers and organizers in Indonesia and El Salvador as well as in New York and Los Angeles. Antiwar activists protesting the U.S. invasion of Iraq coordinated demonstrations of millions of people in scores of countries in the same global spirit.

A NEW GENERATION
OF REGIME CHANGERS

You may be surprised to hear it but—in a sign of a generational awakening—regime change movements are sprouting up on campuses all over the country.

At Boston College, the university at which I teach, a movement called the Global Justice Project (GJP) has been growing for the past five years. It is a bit like MoveOn on campus, a loose network of hundreds of activist students who communicate with each other largely through the Internet. The group formed around the time of the antiglobalization movements in Seattle and takes up issues ranging from sweatshops to fair-trade coffee to peace in the Middle East to the wages of custodians on campus or the uses of the university's billion-dollar endowment. The students have a global perspective, since many of them come to the group after doing service projects in the shanty towns of El Salvador or Mexico.

The students are committed and full of hope. Each year their numbers grow, and they become more sophisticated in using the Internet and the "network" to increase their clout on and off campus. In the current electoral season, most are passionately against Bush, and while many are working for the Democrats, they are looking for more systemic change.

This student politics is rarely reported in the media, but activist regime change groups exist on virtually every major campus in the country and are building a national student network increasingly aligned with broader activist networks around the world. United Students on Sweatshops, speaking on just one issue, has more than two hundred campus chapters. It was from these networks that the millions of antiwar activists appeared, seemingly out of nowhere, and that the global justice movements since Seattle have continued to recruit the global whirlwind of protestors at WTO or International Monetary Fund (IMF) meetings every year. Some of these students go on to work in social change careers that allow them to make a life of social justice. Student activists are the backbone of a generation that will ultimately create regime change.

You may wonder why you don't know about the activist

student generation. Well, here's one reason. Fox News called me to do an interview on a story about student politics today. I agreed, and I told them my observations about the vast proliferation of campus activist groups on my own campus, in Boston, and around the country. But Fox ran its own precooked story line, which said that this was the apathetic, conservative generation. They ran a very short clip of my interview, but it didn't carry my message at all. I guess they didn't want you to hear it.

ALL TOGETHER NOW

Noam Chomsky, who has had his finger on the pulse of American activism since the Vietnam War, observes that grassroots progressive action today surpasses in scope what we saw in the 1960s.[10] Most activists I know agree. Hundreds of insurgent local labor groups, such as Janitors for Justice, represent a generation of multicultural activist workers pushing unions to become a social justice movement, and they are winning major battles for some of the most low-paid workers in the country. Groups like Janitors for Justice, backed by highly politicized unions such as the Service Employees International Union (SEIU) and representing immigrants, women, and workers of color, are a powerful force helping to change the labor establishment in Washington. At rallies to support Janitors for Justice, the size, spirit, and diversity of the crowds on the streets reminds me of the civil rights protests in the 1960s. Had Martin Luther King, Jr., survived, he would be at the front of the barricades again, leading black, brown, and white workers in a multicultural coalition struggling for civil and workers' rights against the third corporate regime.

ADD DEMOCRACY TO THE
DEMOCRATIC PARTY, THEN STIR

As I write this, John Kerry is the anointed Democratic candidate. I'll send him the following letter.

Dear John F. Kerry,

Congratulations on your race to become the Democratic candidate in 2004. Though you are a Washington insider, you are the one who proclaimed, "What we need now is not just a regime change in Saddam Hussein and Iraq, but we need a regime change in the United States." That idea is crucial not only to beating Bush but to changing the country as president. I hope you make it your campaign slogan, and fight for true regime change here at home.

You had a great line in your New Hampshire victory speech. "I have a message for the influence peddlers, for the polluters, the HMOs, the big drug companies that get in the way, the big oil and the special interests who now call the White House their home: we're coming, you're going, and don't let the door hit you on the way out."

I hope you mean it.

You won't beat Bush unless people feel that you truly share their outrage about the war and their disgust that poverty is increasing, that forty-five million Americans have no health care, that job security and wages are dropping like a stone when corporations are getting fatter and more corrupt. Millions of Americans are fed up; they hate Bush and the corporate establishment, but they don't believe in the Democrats either. If they believe you will shake up politics and the Democratic Party—and that you will work to change this horrific, dying regime

and bring the nation back to its democratic principles—
then you've got a chance to turn out millions of new
voters and make history.

Sincerely,

Charles Derber

While grassroots citizen social movements are the heart
and soul of regime change, ending the current regime also
depends on the transformation of the Democratic Party,
which will require a new relationship between the movements and the party itself. During the two prior corporate
regimes, the Democratic party almost became extinct. In
both eras, the Democrats were largely copycat parties of
the Republicans, and voters decided to vote for the real
thing.

Let us be clear. If we are lucky enough to squeak out a
Democratic victory in 2004, it is not going to change the
regime until the Democrats change themselves—or, more
accurately, are forced to change by public opinion mobilized by the social movements. Under the tutelage of the
current Democratic Party establishment, a Democratic
president such as John Kerry will curb the excesses of the
Bush years, moving toward greater multilateralism and
small increases in social security at home. Dean helped
infuse some populist rhetoric into all of the Democratic
candidates' 2004 campaigns. But we cannot expect to see
any systemic weakening of corporate power by the current
Democratic Party. As the structural crises deepen, the
Democrats will be blamed rather than the Republicans,
and workers will become even more disenchanted with
politics, seeing that a change in party does little for them.
Democratic partisans will pop open the Champagne bottles, but it will be a short-lived euphoria.

Franklin Delano Roosevelt offers the lesson that the Democratic Party has to absorb. Roosevelt was the most popular Democratic president in U.S. history and the only one elected for four terms. He did not follow the centrist formula prescribed by today's mainstream Democratic establishment, nor did he accept the idea that the Democratic Party could survive only by making its peace with the reigning corporate elites. While FDR was no revolutionary and should have pushed for deeper and more visionary change, he became the greatest Democratic president by transforming the Democrats into a fiery party dedicated to regime change. He aligned the party with the rising social movements that helped make the Democrats a force for social justice, even as he became hated by much of the corporate establishment as a "class traitor."

You can pretty easily tell the difference between the "democratic" Democrats and those speaking for the corporate regime:

CORPORATE DEMOCRAT: Senator Joe Lieberman
REGIME CHANGE DEMOCRAT: Senator Robert Byrd
CORPORATE DEMOCRAT: Senator John Breaux
REGIME CHANGE DEMOCRAT: Senator Paul Wellstone
CORPORATE DEMOCRAT: Senator Joseph Biden
REGIME CHANGE DEMOCRAT: Representative Dennis Kucinich

The Democratic Party must break with the corporate establishment and reconnect with its populist, progressive, and New Deal legacies, with a far bolder agenda. Democratic Party pollster Stanley Greenberg says that the Democrats will win only with "a base strategy." We must return with a new and more radical spirit to the ideologically charged themes of the Roosevelt years, with hope-giving and ambitious programs for systemic change tied to blistering attacks on corporate greed, the wealth gap, and the destruction of jobs. Greenberg notes that the base is "where you are able to produce voters"[11]—really an argument that the Democratic candidate in 2004 must think, speak, and act like a regime changer.

Democrats such as John Kerry should learn from FDR and the Republicans. Matthew Dowd, a senior advisor to the Bush 2004 reelection team, says of his party, "There's a realization, having looked at the past few elections, that the party that motivates their base—that makes their base emotional and turn out—has a much higher chance of success on Election Day." Bush and the Republican Party have steered hard right in that spirit, as Reagan did in the 1980s. In 2004 and beyond, the Democratic establishment, which has been racing in the same rightward regime direction, must stop abandoning the base voters whose passion it needs to retake the White House and start cultivating the roses growing on its home turf.[12]

DONKEY MOVEON

Here's a wild idea. The Democratic Party becomes a grassroots social movement. Can this happen? Can we make it happen?

OK, we can all dream, you say. But the Democratic Party simply must become the authentic party of democracy, and that means being more than a professional bureaucracy. Bureaucracies get the trains to run on time, but they don't inspire the passion of We, the People. And if we aren't inspired, the Democratic Party won't win or change the regime.

You're probably thinking that the Democratic Party won't become a social movement. You may be right. The corporate cast of the current Democratic Party has created a huge gulf between the movements and the party, one that will never be closed. But the movements and the party need each other now to create regime change. The movements lack the financial and political resources to create regime change without the Democrats representing them. And without the movements, the Democratic Party will be unable to generate the populist vision and connection with the grass roots necessary to win. Howard Dean must have an inkling of this, since it was the grass roots that gave him his early momentum. John Kerry and other candidates all embraced a populist rhetoric when they saw it was lighting up the grass roots. John Edwards's mantra was his critique of "two Americas, one for the privileged few and the other for everyone else."

Many movements have lost all faith in the Democratic Party and are casting their lots with third parties like the Greens, which look a lot like social movements. Representing the Green Party in 2000, Ralph Nader expressed the feeling of many movement activists when he argued correctly that both Bush and Gore would support the corporate regime and that the Democratic Party was a waste of time. Building new parties is an important way to bring ideas into the political arena and mobilize some of the disaffected majority. It is also not necessarily at odds with Democratic Party prospects, since some of the newly mobilized voters may choose to vote for a third party on a local ballot and for a Democrat for president. In many states, such as New York, fusion tickets allow third parties to support a mainstream party candidate for national office while running their own candidates for state and local offices.

Social movements are the most important vehicles for educating the American public about the possibilities of regime change at home. Third parties are but one form of social movement that can help change the political landscape; *social movements—not the Democratic Party or even third parties—will be the real engine of regime change.* The Democratic Party has a major role, but as I said at the beginning of this chapter, it will have to be dragged kicking and screaming by the social movements, and by the pressure of third parties, to the point that Democratic Party politicians have no choice but to ride the popular wave toward regime change. In Chapter 10, I discuss the vision, already arising from the social movements, that will be the alternative to a corporate future. In the final chapter, I describe the far-reaching political realignment that can and must again occur in America to help make regime change a reality. It starts today with the theme of *No Bush Lite,* a slogan that every Democratic Party official and candidate should be forced to repeat like a mantra many times a day. But it will end only with the reality of *No Democracy Lite,* a theme at the heart of regime change and of the regime to come.

CHAPTER 10

A NEW, OLD ROAD MAP FOR CHANGE

We need regime change at home quickly, but it won't happen until we know where we want to go. This requires big thinking by social movements, the Democratic Party, and especially readers like you. A new regime, as I'm sure you've concluded, cannot just be token reform of the corporate order. It has to be driven by a truly bold vision based on America's own core values.

All corporate regimes transfer sovereignty away from the people. Our third corporate regime has been extreme, with transnational corporations unashamedly hijacking our government for their own ends. This has been accompanied by a disastrous loss of citizen empowerment and social security. The next regime must return sovereignty to the people in a democracy tailored for the new century, what I call "New Democracy."

TAKE DOWN THE PILLARS OF THE THIRD CORPORATE REGIME

I'll bet you're already skeptical, and I can understand why. It's hard to take seriously the very idea of democracy—old or new—in a globalized era of transnational companies, corporate-dominated campaign financing, corporate-owned media, two corporate political parties, a military-industrial complex, and curtailed civil liberties. New Democracy can work only if it is inspiring enough to turn a population of exhausted workers and cynical couch potatoes into active citizens who believe they can make a better world.

This is a government of the people, by the people, for the people no longer. It is a government of corporations, by corporations, for corporations.[1]

PRESIDENT RUTHERFORD B. HAYES, *speaking of the first corporate regime*

It's a tall order, but we have a history suggesting that it is possible. The Populists, progressives, and New Dealers all had to refashion democracy in the face of their own corporate regimes. They succeeded in regime change. If they could do it, we can too. New Democracy requires that you and I get together to take down the pillars of the third corporate regime, pillars that have become huge hurdles to citizen action and to democracy itself. Recall the house this regime built and the long shadows cast by its pillars.

The **corporation** itself, the first, and ultimate, pillar of

PULL 'EM DOWN

Pillar 1—The Transnational Corporation
*Turns us from active citizens into entertained,
passively managed, and, yes, brainwashed consumers*

Pillar 2—Corpocracy
*Turns Washington, D.C., over to corporate raiders
who are running your government for their profits*

Pillar 3—Social Insecurity
*Forces most of us to spend our days running in place
just to survive, anxious about whether we can pay
the bills, get affordable housing and health care,
and afford retirement*

Pillar 4—Empire
*Builds American military power while undermining
relations with our allies, breeding more hatred of
Americans around the world, and decreasing our
national security*

Pillar 5—The Corporate Mystique
*Promotes the ideology of freedom while robbing us
of the values and capacity to escape our condition
as servants of the corporate order*

the current regime, must be reconstructed in the coming order. New Democracy is based on "corporate abolitionism," which transforms the current corporate model of business enterprise. *Corporate abolitionism does not mean demonizing or abolishing business, even big business, but*

it means eliminating business's antidemocratic features.
We need to change the DNA of today's corporation, which
has become inherently political, parasitical, and predatory.
We also have to limit the exit power of corporations that
subordinates countries to companies.

Abolishing the current corporate structure is a long-
term goal, but we must make it a central aim, educating our
fellow citizens about the ways in which corporations are
deadly to both market competition and democracy. It is not
just the ripped-off workers at Enron who need a more accountable business system: we all do.

As I spelled out in the Introduction, the current regime
is based on a horrific corporate/government marriage that
dominates America. The new regime must decisively end
corporate domination of politics, that is, it must dismantle
corpocracy, the second pillar of the current regime. Senator John McCain gained instant political support by proclaiming in his 2000 campaign that getting big money out
of politics was his top priority. Campaign finance reform,
he said, "is a fight to take our government back from the
powerbrokers and special interests, and return it to the
people and the noble cause of freedom it was created to
serve."[2] Amen!

A third regime pillar that must go is **social insecurity**,
a consequence of the corporate rollback of the health, education, and worker protections created by the New Deal.
Social insecurity is where politics gets personal for ordinary people. The third corporate regime has delivered a

*There can be no effective control of corporations while
their political activity remains. To put an end to it
will be neither a short nor easy task but it can be done.*

THEODORE ROOSEVELT,[3] *1910*

severe, sustained kick in the stomach to millions of poor, working, and middle-class Americans who live under conditions of temporary, outsourced employment and downsized services. We're all feeling the pain in one way or another.

If the New Deal could help save Americans during the Depression, we can create a new model of social security today. As observed in Chapters 2 and 3, the New Deal ended partly because it was too timid, failing to deliver the real security that all Americans of every race, age, and gender needed. We must ensure that all of us can live without fear of chronic or catastrophic job loss, of wages that do not bring us out of poverty, of a bankrupt public education and health system, and of air or water that can make us ill.

A fourth pillar of the current regime that must go is **empire**. The impetus toward expansion runs deep in U.S. history but is at odds with the Founders' view of the nation. Empire and democracy are irreconcilable, and the regime's foreign policy is leading to anti-Americanism endangering the security of every American.

BUSH IS NUMBER 2

In November 2003, the *New York Times* reported that "in an opinion poll of 7,000 Europeans conducted recently by the European Commission in Brussels, respondents ranked Bush the number two threat to world peace, tied with North Korean leader Kim Jong II and behind Prime Minister Ariel Sharon of Israel."[4]

New Democracy has deep American roots, but it can emerge only with a transformation of culture and values. The third corporate regime has enshrined the **corporate mystique**, its fifth pillar, which helps support all the rest. Its remarkable accomplishment has been to create among so many of us the illusion that the giant American corporation and citizen democracy go hand in hand.

New Democracy is based on values of citizen empowerment rather than corporate sovereignty. The third corporate regime speaks the rhetoric of citizenship but transforms it into the art of consumerism. The citizen has become a consumer of politics as entertainment, an extension of the passive and privatized culture of the couch potato. Thus the easy rise of Ronald Reagan and now Arnold Schwarzenegger: the actor into politician and the politician into actor. Most of us still believe abstractly in citizen participation, but we don't believe it can make any difference in a corporate world. The mall is where the action is.

BUILDING NEW DEMOCRACY

OK, we're about ready to roll up our sleeves and build some pillars, but first we have to know what they are.

The first pillar of New Democracy is what I call the *Active Citizens' Network.* It is a vast network of all the civic associations, nonprofits, labor unions, NGOs, and social movements in America organized to take back control of the country from big money. The network already exists, and it is huge. In fact, it is bigger and more historically rooted in America than in any other country. You are almost certainly part of the network already! But the network lacks the money and political organization of the

MEET THE PILLARS
OF THE NEW
DEMOCRACY REGIME

Dominant Institution—Active Citizens' Network
*Ordinary citizens get it on in their communities
and in Washington, D.C.*

Mode of Politics—New Democracy
Ordinary people like you and me actually run the house.

Social Contract—Real Social Security
The tenants get ownership and legal protection.

Foreign Policy—Collective Security
The house helps create a neighborhood association.

Ideology—Citizen Empowerment
The house walks its freedom talk.

transnational firms. Regime change will take place when civil society—meaning you, me, and others in the network—organize ourselves to eclipse the corporations as the dominant force in America. If your skepticism is rising again, remember, collectively, we are the overwhelming majority.

The political aim of the Active Citizens' Network is to replace corpocracy with New Democracy, an idea really as American as apple pie. I call it *new* only because there are new hurdles to democracy in an age of global corporations. We, as citizens, now have to take back control of *our* businesses, *our* media, *our* educational and health systems, and, ultimately, the Democratic Party and our federal government itself. It's the right thing to do.

Active citizens will seek regime change for self-interested reasons: our own real social security, the third pillar of New Democracy. Every regime change requires rewriting the social contract, in this case moving toward a social order that rewards ordinary citizens like you with health care, education, secure jobs, living wages, and other forms of social well-being. Couch potatoes will get off their rear ends and into the political sphere at the prospect of a better and more secure life for themselves and their families. Won't you fight for your own social security? Won't your neighbors?

Self-interest will also drive the construction of the fourth pillar of the new regime: collective security. We Americans will be safe only when we fight for a world of international cooperation and law, something that presidents from George Washington to Franklin Roosevelt to Dwight Eisenhower all urged as the American way. In a globalized economy, democracy and safety at home depend on renouncing unilateralism and turning toward cooperation with other nations.

Finally, all this obviously depends on empowerment of ordinary citizens—meaning, again, you. The current regime depends, as just noted, on your passivity and disbelief in the possibility of regime change. Cultural change cannot be legislated, but the idea that you and all other citizens have the right and responsibility to be active in government is what the Constitution is all about. I hope you still believe in it!

THE NEW DEMOCRACY PROGRAM

Below I outline a bold New Democracy platform for regime change. It pushes the envelope, as do all regime change agendas. The New Deal ideas of government regulation, powerful labor unions, and Social Security would have looked totally utopian in the late 1920s under the second corporate regime, and they took decades to implement. Some of the ideas here may seem equally unrealistic, and they will have to be implemented in small steps through a long reform process. **But I offer here the recipe for real regime change, and the ingredients should help business become more efficient as well as more accountable.**

"Take the country back from big business and create a new government, of, by, and for the people." This is the preamble tying all of my New Democracy proposals together. The American creed is one person, one vote—not one dollar, one vote. Corporations have stolen our government, and it is time for you and me to reclaim it.

REWRITE CORPORATE CHARTERS TO ENSURE THAT BUSINESS SERVES THE PUBLIC, RATHER THAN VICE VERSA

Corporate charters are the state laws defining corporate rights and obligations. The idea of them may make your eyes glaze over, but a charter is a corporate constitution, and what it says affects *your* freedom, *your* well-being, and *your* happiness. We need to return to the vision of the Founders, who proclaimed that corporations are businesses created by the public to serve the public interest.

James W. Rouse, founder of The Rouse Company, writes, "Profit is not the legitimate purpose of business. The purpose is to provide a service needed by society."[5] Even though Rouse is a CEO, his idea is identical to that of the Founders. The earliest corporate charters stated that corporations must ensure the public interest and be directly accountable to the citizens' representatives in state legislatures. Today's charter should legally redefine big business as a public entity with three chartered missions:

I see in the near future a crisis approaching that unnerves me and causes me to tremble for the safety of my country . . . corporations have enthroned and an era of corruption in high places will follow and the money power of the country will endeavor to prolong its reign by working upon the prejudices of the people until all wealth is aggregated in a few hands and the Republic is destroyed.[6]

ABRAHAM LINCOLN, *1864*

to serve the public and
   be accountable to it
to return profit to
   shareholders
to protect workers,
   consumers, and other
   stakeholders, including
   the environment and
   democracy itself

Although weakened by three corporate regimes, the concept of a public mission for the corporation still resonates in American law. Broadcast companies today, since they operate on public airwaves, are expected to abide by legal public interest standards requiring fair access, community programming, transparency in financial sponsorship, diversity of ownership, and other major considerations.[7] Similar public interest standards should be written and enforced for all big business and enshrined in their charters.

Rewriting charters is not as radical as it sounds. Thirty-one states have already changed their corporate chartering legislation to permit directors to make decisions that benefit all stakeholders, a first step on the road to New Democracy. Such chartering reform requires two other major steps.

> Charters should require directors to take into account the interests of the public at large, as well as the interests of stakeholders such as workers.
>
> In the new global economy, we need charters to establish enforceable codes of conduct at the global and national, as well as state, levels. We should retain state charters but also have limited provisions within federal and U.N. authority governing corporations at higher levels. Otherwise, corporations will simply exit to other states or countries where they can abuse the public interest as they please!

STRIP CORPORATIONS OF CONSTITUTIONAL RIGHTS THAT BELONG ONLY TO FLESH AND BLOOD CITIZENS

Regime change requires a conversation about fundamentals: in this case, the Constitution of the United States. Thomas Jefferson would roll over in his grave if he knew that presidents are appointing judges who are awarding corporations protections under the Bill of Rights, including the First, Fourth, Fifth, Sixth, Seventh, and Fourteenth Amendments.

You can have a constitution that protects real citizens or a constitution that protects corporations, but not both. This is a point that the Founders understood well, and it explains why the word "corporation" never appears in the Constitution. Corporations were never awarded constitutional protections until the robber barons stacked the Supreme Court in the first corporate regime.

It was not until the 1886 Santa Clara case that the robber baron Supreme Court defined corporations as legal persons with constitutional protections. It's time to reverse this egregious decision if we want to protect our own rights. Today, corporate constitutional rights erode our rights in the name of protecting them. The corporate right to speech (where speech is seen as political donations) is defined by this regime as essential to the free speech of all citizens, but it diminishes the rights of you and me by drowning the political debate in corporate money. There is nothing more important to New Democracy than campaign finance reform that leads toward complete public financing of campaigns, as is the case in most European societies.

Here's what we urgently have to do. We need to reassert, through federal legislation, that corporations are not legal persons protected under the Bill of Rights. Most important, they do not have First Amendment protections to give unlimited political contributions, a restriction on corporations that the Supreme Court affirmed as recently as its 2003 upholding of the McCain-Feingold Act for campaign finance reform.

Business enterprises deserve clear, legally enforceable rights, but not those in the Bill of Rights intended to protect live citizens like you and me. An example close to home: District Court Judge Edward Nottingham in 2003 threw out the Do Not Call Registry that allowed individuals to opt out of unwanted phone solicitations because it allegedly violated corporate rights to free speech. Only when corporations are denied constitutional protection under the First Amendment can we enjoy uninterrupted dinners and our own rights to privacy. Millions of Americans realize this and are working for complete public financing of campaigns; scores of active citizens' groups seek to abolish corporate personhood in their own states.[8]

GET CORPORATIONS OUT OF POLITICS FOR GOOD

Corporations larger than most countries snuff out democracy, and we need to restrain them with strong regulations and every creative initiative you can think of. I would start with the following political changes:

> In addition to public financing of campaigns, work on every other campaign reform initiative that drains the swamp of corporate money in Washington.
>
> Curb corporate lobbying, and restrict the right of industries to draft laws governing themselves.
>
> Outlaw use of shareholder funds for political causes.
>
> Prevent former high-level politicians from becoming business lobbyists for at least ten years.
>
> Prevent former or present high-level corporate officers from serving on commissions regulating their respective industries.
>
> Criminalize threats by corporate officials to influence employees' votes.

Rescind the "investor rights" clauses of trade agreements, which allow foreign corporations to sue governments for passing labor or environmental laws.

Penalize corporations that explicitly extort political concessions by threatening to leave a state or country.

Limit corporate subsidies that can be poured back into influencing votes in Washington.

We also need to rewire the corporation to make it more attuned to public concerns. We can start breaking up some of the world's biggest companies, like Wal-Mart, which is bigger than 161 countries. We need an antitrust policy that busts trusts whose very size makes them dangerous for democracy.

We also must make big business more participatory and democratic, both to make it more efficient and to align its interests with the public good. More than ten thousand companies have employee stock-ownership plans, and workers in many of the largest companies already have enough company stock in their pension funds to be a pivotal bloc. Workers in Germany, even if they own no stock, are guaranteed 50 percent of the seats on their company's board because they are viewed as the key stakeholders. In the United States, we need a corporate board that is one-third workers, one-third shareholders, and one-third public representatives. This make-up would help align the corporation's politics with the common good, and since it would give workers a stake in the company, it would also increase loyalty, efficiency, and productivity.

PASS LAWS TO PREVENT CORPORATIONS FROM OWNING AND RUNNING SCHOOLS, HEALTH CARE FACILITIES, MILITARY SERVICES, AND THE MASS MEDIA

Democracy and active citizenship require that public services remain public. This is a very simple idea, consistent with the original U.S. constitutional framework, but it has been severely eroded over the course of three corporate regimes.

Privatizing everything from education to medical care to prisons leaves a shriveled public sector and transfers the most important powers of the people from government to corporations. The business of the people must reside where the Constitution requires, in civil society and the hallowed halls of democratic government. Corporations must be constitutionally prevented from owning and running the sources of information on which democracy depends, especially the mass media and the educational system.

Regime change is emerging as a battle between "privateers," who seek to put a "for sale" sign on anything profitable, and "public guardians," the active citizens who are trying to preserve the vital public sector essential to democracy. The battle to preserve a vital public media has already become intense, as a few giant corporations,

The true friend of property, the true conservative, is he who insists that property shall be the servant and not the master of the common-wealth; who insists that the creature of man's making shall be the servant, not the master, of the man who made it. The citizens of the United States must effectively control the mighty commercial forces which they themselves have called into being.[9]

THEODORE ROOSEVELT, *1907*

such as Fox, AOL–Time Warner, and Clear Channel, have used their influence on the Federal Communications Commission (FCC) to privatize and deregulate the media further, allowing conglomerates to monopolize media markets in your town and across the planet. When MoveOn launched a petition campaign to reverse the FCC edict, hundreds of thousands of grassroots citizens sent emails and made phone calls to Washington, forcing the Senate to block the FCC ruling. Thus began a battle for control of the media that will spread to ownership of the schools, the health care system, and the government itself.

PUT AN END TO CORPORATE GLOBALIZATION IN A GLOBAL ECONOMY REGULATED BY GLOBAL CITIZENS

One reader told me, "Yeah, fine, but U.S. corporations can simply move their headquarters to another country if they fear that a regime change here will undermine their ability to maximize profits or dominate Washington." She is right.

We, the citizens, can prevent this only through global regulation of international investment to keep giant companies from terrorizing poor (and rich) countries with constant threats to leave. Here's how to help stop this:

Tax short-term, speculative global investment.
Give favorable tax treatment to long-term global
    investors.
Write global corporate charters with codes of conduct
    enforceable by the United Nations and regional
    authorities, as well as by national governments.
Adopt global labor and environmental protections at
    the heart of trade treaties.

Offer debt relief to empower poor nations.
Create democratically structured new global trade and
financing authorities.

If global companies know that they will have to respect labor and the environment wherever they go; that they will have to answer to the public in every country; that they are required by a global charter to be accountable to the workers in every free-trade zone; that they will have to pay taxes in every host country to ensure that they contribute to social development; and that they will face global consumer and judicial sanctions if they abuse the public trust, we will know we have begun to achieve a global regime change that sustains regime change at home.

The WTO, IMF, and World Bank are the corporate regime's global handmaidens, and regime change requires that we trade them in for more democratic and transparent entities protecting workers and the environment in both rich and poor nations. The money changers in the temple are now global, and we can have no regime change at home without planetary regime change that puts people before profit and global citizens' networks at the helm of the global economy. This means that global NGOs, global social movements, and democratic states will replace global corporations as the stewards of the global economy.

PASS LAWS TO GUARANTEE AMERICANS FOOD, HOUSING, MEDICAL CARE, EDUCATION, JOBS, AND A LIVING WAGE

You have a human and legal right to real social security, according to the U.N. 1948 Declaration of Human Rights,

which the United States helped draft and signed. Only the manipulations of the current regime have made these social rights seem like socialism, when in fact they are embraced by market societies all over the world and simply ensure that Americans will get the decent education, health care, affordable housing, and secure retirement that Franklin D. Roosevelt saw as the American birthright.

We must guarantee that every child can live free of poverty and can access good education, that every worker is entitled to a living wage, and that you and every other citizen are assured health care and retirement security. Universal health care is a high immediate priority. Polls suggest that Americans increasingly favor universal health care, a barometer of the desire of Americans for real social security.

When computer programmers as well as auto workers are seeing their jobs disappear overseas, Americans need a regime change guaranteeing them the means to a livelihood. Full employment was the core social security policy of the New Deal, and in the global economy we need it more than ever. Put unemployed, underemployed, outsourced, and temped Americans to work building schools, clinics, or roads and serving old people, children, and other needy or abandoned citizens. FDR, Lyndon Johnson, and even Richard Nixon argued for a minimum income and for work for all.

The United Nations has affirmed that everyone has a basic human right to a job that pays a living wage. The U.N. Declaration of Human Rights declares that "Everyone who works has the right to just and favourable remuneration ensuring for himself [sic] and his [sic] family an existence worthy of human dignity."[10] In 1891, Pope Leo XIII, in his famed encyclical on "the rights of labor," proclaimed the right of the worker to a job with dignity and a living wage, a principle that has been reaffirmed by the Catholic Church ever since.[11] *It is time that America caught up with the United Nations and the pope.*

HEALTH CARE FOR ALL

According to a 1998 NBC/*Wall Street Journal* poll, 67 percent of the public support a guarantee of health coverage for all Americans, regardless of health or employment status.

RENOUNCE EMPIRE, END UNILATERAL WARS, AND EMBRACE COLLECTIVE SECURITY

The Iraq debacle and the disastrous impact of the current regime's effort to dominate the world should set the nation on a new foreign policy course. As conservative politician and writer Pat Buchanan has proclaimed, we were founded as "a Republic, not an Empire."[12] Our Constitution and democratic spirit, and perhaps the survival of the world, require that we stay that way.

We should abandon our imperial foreign policy and embrace the United Nations that we helped build. We must now work with our allies to build a robust system of international law and multilateral peacekeeping, signing on to the International Criminal Court, nonproliferation and arms agreements, and funding for a permanent U.N. peacekeeping constabulary. Such multilateralism is necessary to keep the world from blowing itself up, to end our long sponsorship of state terrorist regimes I discuss in Chapter 4, to end anti-Americanism, and to preserve our own democracy.

> *Observe good faith and justice toward all nations. Cultivate peace and harmony with all.*[13]
>
> PRESIDENT WASHINGTON, *in his 1796 farewell address*

When we renounce empire, we can massively reduce U.S. spending on nuclear and conventional weapons. We can also withdraw most U.S. forces from Europe and other parts of the world, close U.S. bases abroad, and commit our forces mainly to international and regional peacekeeping efforts under U.N. authority. By radically downsizing the military, we can pay down our looming debt and reinvest in social security at home. The conversion from a war economy to a peaceful one should have begun right after World War II, or certainly after the Cold War, but it is not too late. Renouncing empire will help remedy the economic and moral damage that U.S. warrior politics has caused to the rest of the world and to ourselves.

The U.S. "war on terrorism" will be no more effective than its war on drugs. Terrorists have been redefined as anyone opposing U.S. interests, and our war on terrorism ignores the state terrorist regimes that we support, including Saddam Hussein's when he was our ally. When defined properly as those who use violence against civilians for political causes, terrorists can best be dealt with by dealing with their legitimate political grievances. Terrorists who refuse political negotiation or political solutions can be tracked and apprehended mainly through the cooperation of human intelligence operatives in the countries where they operate. The only way to keep us and our communities safe is through a multilateral diplomatic partnership, led by the United Nations and regional security networks, to track funding, share intelligence, and seek resolution to the political crises that give rise to terrorism.

In the councils of government, we must guard against the acquisition of unwarranted influence, whether sought or unsought, by the military-industrial complex.[14]

PRESIDENT EISENHOWER,
in his 1961 farewell address

END OUR RUSH TO 1984, AND
PRESERVE OUR CIVIL LIBERTIES

The war on terrorism is aimed as much at undermining civil liberties and active citizenship as it is at stopping terrorists. It is the umbrella for the new surveillance state, which not only suspends constitutional rights for any terrorist "suspect," but seeks to collect information on you by snooping on emails, snail mail, course curricula, credit cards, and book-borrowing from libraries, and by installing video cameras in public and private space. Civil liberties are at the heart of active citizenship, and they are the essential foundation of both citizen empowerment and New Democracy.

The Patriot Act should be repealed, and its sequel, "Son of Patriot," should be denounced, making clear that these acts are the prelude to an Orwellian future at home as well as overseas. In times of crisis, we need to extend rather than slash and burn our constitutional freedoms by embracing the protections of the International Criminal Court and many U.N. covenants on the rights of workers, children, women, and immigrants. You might be next on the regime's list of targets.

ANSWERS TO YOUR
HARD-NOSED QUESTIONS

The steps toward a New Democracy are appealing, but what are the trade-offs? Can these changes ever be achieved in America? They cannot, in fact, be achieved in the current regime, and it will take regime change based on a major political realignment to make it happen over many years. In Chapter 11, I look at how that realignment can take place. First, though, I look at other tough questions you may have about the practicality, trade-offs, and costs of this vision.

Q: HOW CAN YOU ARGUE FOR CORPORATE ABOLITIONISM WHEN CORPORATIONS HAVE PRODUCED THE GREATEST PROSPERITY IN HISTORY?

A: Corporations have undoubtedly contributed to progress by amassing the vast amount of capital required for innovation and production in capital-intensive industries. They have also created a cheap consumer culture that is the envy of the planet. Corporations are the symbols of American power and wealth.

But this corporate triumph, as I have shown, derives largely from corporations' success using *your* taxpayer money and *your* government to *their* own ends. Your government created the limited liability that allows corporations to concentrate vast capital with minimal risk, and it pays for the huge, public research and development effort that generates basic discoveries. Your government trains the corporate labor force, pays for highways and ports that corporations use, discourages unionism, shapes the macroeconomic policies that stabilize the inherently cyclical instability of the market, and pays for the environmental, social, and human costs that corporations acting as cold cash registers leave in their wake. We have to create a business system that does not drain the federal treasury, steal from the poor, and ravage the social order to promote the economy.

Corporations are huge command systems, a bit like the failed communist states or the hierarchies of the medieval church, that concentrate power and wealth among unaccountable leaders. They win monopolies through price gouging, political favors, collusive alliances, and other anticompetitive strategies that erode efficiency. They discourage worker productivity not only by making workers disposable, but also by legally disenfranchising them; only shareholders have legal claims on corporate profit or control.

By breaking up the biggest monopolies and rewriting the charter to empower workers and other stakeholders, we create a more open, inclusive, entrepreneurial, and accountable organization whose DNA is now socially wired. That wiring cuts workers into governance and thereby increases loyalty and productivity, and it reduces the social and political costs of a corrupt inner circle that cannot run the organization profitably without looting its own workers and the rest of society.

We need to retain the parts of the business order that yield economic efficiency and innovation, while changing the anticompetitive, hierarchical, and deeply politicized corporate elements that are destructive for the economy as well as for democracy and society. Most jobs are generated in the small and midsize business sector where genuine entrepreneurship still exists. New Democracy would encourage these forms of business and create more of them by encouraging worker-owned firms and other local or democratic businesses.

Q: BUT AREN'T WE TALKING, NONETHELESS, ABOUT REDUCING ECONOMIC GROWTH AND PROSPERITY FOR SOCIAL, POLITICAL, OR MORAL ENDS?

A: The answer is yes and no. No, because, as just noted, the corporate system achieves short-term growth at such high social, environmental, and political costs that it cannot sustain growth in the long term. Because of the greater inherent efficiency of the new democratic, competitive business model, it can equal or surpass long-term growth performance of the corporate model.

But yes, New Democracy does not prioritize economic growth as its highest value; instead, the preservation of society and democracy itself is its most basic aim. Unfettered economic growth in already affluent nations is likely to be unsustainable environmentally. And if trade-offs are required between a higher level of growth or a higher level of democracy, New Democracy chooses the latter.

Sustainable growth remains important because of the desperate condition of three-fourths of the world, and because growth can generate major revenue for alleviating poverty and creating jobs at home. The European economic model, which has similarities to New Democracy, shows that growth, productivity, and global competitiveness are all consistent with a social contract emphasizing democracy and social security. The Europeans have had less than ideal growth rates because their own system has bureaucratic and corporatist elements. The new U.S. order would be more flexible and participatory, committed to the maximum sustainable growth consistent with democracy.

A: Unlike Europe, the United States, since its founding, has emphasized limited government in its political discourse. However, beginning with the first regime, in which Hamilton's policies triumphed over Jefferson's more populist proposals, a larger government devoted to commercial interests won the day. This helps explain the contradictions of the conversation about "limited government" in America today. Corporations continue to emphasize the Founders' rhetoric of limited government, but in practice they have built, and depend on, big government. If we cut through the rhetoric, the real issue is not the size of government, since both the corporations and their opponents have supported and required a sizeable government apparatus, but rather the ends to which it is put.

Today, corporations are the architects of America's biggest government ever and the highest-ever deficits. This extremism has been necessary to bail them out and sate their greed, but it shows the absurdity of the corporate rhetoric about their love of limited government. Ironically, the proposals above would eliminate a huge chunk of government spending on corporate welfare and militarism, and they could be presented to the public as a far more effective defense of limited government than what the corporations offer.

Regime change will require making sure that the vision of social security and New Democracy is genuinely not a recipe for stealing away personal freedoms. Genuine tensions arise between universal government programs and personal choice, so an American social security has to be tailored to maximize flexibility and choice. Federally funded social programs should be administered locally with maximum citizen and community involvement. As for whether higher taxes translate into less liberty, it is worth going back to Adam Smith, who noted that capitalism depended on the existence of a sustainable community of people who care about and trust each other. It is true that absolute freedom can be maximized in the short term by keeping all of one's earnings for oneself. But in the long run, there will be no earnings to keep or make if the community around you falls apart. As William C. Norris, the founder of Control Data Corporation, writes, "You can't do business in a society that's burning."[15]

Q: I STILL FEEL THAT YOUR AGENDA HAS A "PIE IN THE SKY" FEELING. WHAT MAKES YOU BELIEVE THAT THIS SEA-CHANGE IN AMERICA IS POSSIBLE?

A: Can this really happen in America? *Can a nation of couch potatoes become active citizens?* Or are Americans too brainwashed, apathetic, or powerless?

I sometimes feel discouraged myself, despairing about a country whose citizens seem so vulnerable to the seductions of the mall and the manipulations of fear and patriotism from on high. Even though millions of people protested the war in Iraq, most Americans are not in an activist frame of mind. Many work too hard or watch too many sitcoms to think about politics, let alone to try to make social change. Moreover, every regime tries to drum into our heads that things cannot be different, and this one has the electronic media and the big money to indoctrinate the population more than any previous one.

I don't believe these changes are inevitable, but they *are* possible. In fact, the prospects for hope are far stronger than you might think. Here's why:

HISTORY. None of us can read the future, but reliable clues come from our past. As I emphasized earlier, all of our earlier corporate regimes have succumbed to reform movements that created regime change and a better America. If you don't believe regime change is possible now, you are taking the position that history will not repeat itself. This would itself be a first in history! All the historical evidence suggests that regimes are transient; in fact, most do not last more than thirty years. This one is already almost twenty-five years old, and it is showing its age. History tells me that change, if not imminent, is blowing in the wind.

SELF-INTEREST. Americans now work, on average, a month longer than Europeans and get a lower wage and far fewer social benefits. Put simply, most Americans need regime change for selfish reasons. It will improve their job security, their social security, and their quality of life. As the government keeps shoveling pots of money to the wealthy, and the gap between the very rich and everyone else keeps growing, self-interest will lead the majority of Americans to see that this really is a regime of, by, and for corporations.

THE PEOPLE'S HISTORY. Grassroots movements are in the American bloodstream. All you have to do is read Howard Zinn's *A People's History of the United States* to see that this has always been a country of social movements. In fact, you could argue that no country has ever had as many different and powerful social movements as the United States has: abolitionists, suffragists and feminists, civil rights activists, antiwar legions, environmentalists, the labor movement, and the Populists themselves. These movements have always kept the flame of democracy alive in America, and they are very much alive today, more active now and more technologically empowered than probably at any earlier time in history. If you don't believe me, listen to such movement stalwarts as Studs Terkel, Pete Seeger, Noam Chomsky, and Zinn himself, who say the same thing.

TRADITION. The changes I propose sound radical, but they really have a conservative foundation: the Declaration of Independence and the Constitution. We need regime change not to undermine the American creed of democracy but to preserve it. In other words, the regime is out of step with American tradition and regime change is necessary to restore basic American truths. What's radical and extremist is not New Democracy but the sham democracy of the current regime. Regime change is the conservative thing to do today.

THE BIG TENT. Precisely because the regime is violating Americans' heritage of democracy, regime change appeals to Americans across the political spectrum. Regime change always seems radical, thus creating a "pie in the sky" feeling before it happens, but today it is also a conservative impulse. Regime change will increasingly attract Independent and Republican Americans as well as Democrats and progressives. But I have not yet shown that such broad political realignment is possible, and that is why I have written the final chapter. Perhaps it will help you see why regime change is likely to become good old American common sense.

CHAPTER 11

REQUILTING
THE BIG TENT

On November 5, 2003, Democratic presidential candidate Howard Dean got into hot water when he said on the campaign trail, "I still want to be the candidate for guys with Confederate flags on their pickup trucks."[1] The words about the flag were insensitive and poorly chosen, but Dean had an important message: the Democrats cannot win until those guys and gals in the South abandon Bush. Democrats cannot win without a lot of other Independents and conservatives too, nor can they hope for regime change without major realignment.

Political scientists use the term "realignment" to refer to a sweeping shift in the politics and party identification of large groups of Americans.[2] I argued in Chapter 3 that political realignment has historically been key to regime change. President Roosevelt created regime change in the

The only way we're going to beat George Bush is if Southern, white, working families and African American working families come together under the Democratic tent, as they did under FDR.[3] HOWARD DEAN, *Democratic presidential candidate,* 2003

1930s by building a coalition of conservative Southern Democrats, urban Northern Catholic workers, and East Coast liberals and intellectuals. In 1980, Ronald Reagan and the New Right rode to power by putting together a new coalition of Southern conservatives defecting from the New Deal coalition, as well as corporate elites, Christian fundamentalists, and small business proprietors.

Some Republicans, such as Fox News pundit Fred Barnes, have argued that a Bush victory in 2004 would speed realignment toward a new "9/11 majority." If this scenario is correct, the third corporate regime may shift toward an even more extremist one.[4] But I argue here that a progressive regime change is more likely to be in the cards, although it's still in its early stages. In this chapter, I show how such a realignment—despite the formidable hurdles—could be mobilized by the New Democracy agenda described in the previous chapter. I discuss how various constituencies that have been lost to the Republican Party are ripe for realignment because they are betrayed by the current regime, and regime change would serve their interests and values.

CONSERVATIVES: SOUTHERNERS, SMALL BUSINESS, AND PICKUP-TRUCK DADS

The regime has been winning the South by shouting "No new taxes" and "Support our troops," both traditionally popular Southern views. But neoconservatives leading the regime embrace basic policies wildly at odds with traditional conservative values and implement domestic and foreign policies that endanger the economic interests and social well-being of many conservative groups. Southern males with pickups, and their race-car-driving cousins in the working class dubbed "NASCAR dads," are suffering from job loss encouraged by the regime's trade policies. Hundreds of thousands of textile jobs alone, including 316,000 just between 2000 and 2003,[5] have been lost in America under this regime, mainly from the South and mainly a product of the regime's trade policies. Small business all over the country is taking hits from the regime's tax, trade, and regulatory policies that favor corporations over the mom-and-pop store. Southerners are also disproportionately likely to serve and be killed in the regime's foreign military adventurism. Southerners, small business owners, and pickup-truck rural dads thus are victims of what I call the *"betrayal of the conservatives."*

Having cast its lot with transnational corporations, neoconservatism is breeding discontent in its very backyard. Disenchanted elements in the conservative community believe today that the regime has abandoned America itself, seeking instead a global corporate empire, and that it has created a serious violation of national interests that conservatives have always cherished. Pat Buchanan, among the most vocal critics of the party he once belonged to, has repeatedly denounced the regime's policies that are heavily biased in favor of global corporations. Free-trade policies and "American trade shortfall," Buchanan wrote in 1999 in an attack on corporate globalization, exacts "a high human cost (on workers). . . . The leaders of the two Beltway parties speak in one identical voice—'full speed ahead with globalization,' no matter what price paid."[6]

Conservatives have always looked to the Founders for their basic creed. Buchanan can rightly say that the current regime has abandoned that heritage and eroded basic conservative values. George Washington, Thomas Jefferson, James Madison, and other Founders believed that democracy rested on a middle class of small business owners and farmers, and they feared that big corporations would crush the republic. Today, their fears have come true with a vengeance. Corporate globalism supersedes local democracy, corporate monopolies undermine competition, and the lies and deceptions of the third corporate regime make a travesty of conservative principles of morality and integrity. Put simply, CORPORATIONS AREN'T CONSERVATIVE.

All this makes reclaiming the Southern legacy of the New Deal possible but not inevitable. While third-party conservatives like Pat Buchanan and Ross Perot attracted millions of voters, mainstream conservatives are not rushing toward regime change. Bush maintains support of the great majority of Republican voters by his position on a small number of hot-button issues like gun control and abortion, while also using the familiar deceptive rhetoric about limited government, lower taxes, and liberty. September 11 was the ultimate gift that allowed a corporate neoconservative regime to disguise its abandonment of conservative principles under the umbrella of national security.

Nonetheless, the marriage between traditional conservatives and the third corporate regime is tenuous. Buchanan's angry rejection of large transnational corporations has increasing appeal among grassroots conservatives. Over the years, I have spoken on many conservative AM talk radio shows in the South and West, and I have been struck by the level of distrust and anger at corporations and at the surprising resonance between my own populist corporate critique and the conservative mind-set. Conservatives will be reluctant converts, but many are ripe for a New Democracy regime change framed in their own language.

Much of the New Democracy agenda should appeal to them. New Democracy has a conservative foundation in the constitutional concepts of accountable government and a citizen republic. Conservatives and regime changers share a preference for local economies and small business, a critique of corporate globalization and free trade, a demand for ending corporate welfare and corporate tax breaks, and the aim of helping displaced American workers and increasing opportunity for those working hard at low wages. The emphasis on global non-interventionism, and the focus on noncorporate values of community, honesty, and quality of life, are also conservative principles.

THE REAGAN DEMOCRATS: URBAN, ETHNIC, AND IMMIGRANT WORKERS

In 1980, Reagan's presidential victory—a political realignment of major dimensions—created a new concept: the Reagan Democrats. These were the urban, Midwestern, Catholic, blue-collar workers, from Flint, Michigan, to Toledo, Ohio, who had been a core part of the New Deal coalition but swung over to support the Republican Party in the 1980s. Reagan succeeded in regime change because he not only consolidated the new Republican South but also stole from the Democrats their base in the North.

Located in key strategic states like Pennsylvania, Illinois, Michigan, and Ohio, the Reagan Democrats remain one of the most important swing-voting blocs. In the 1990s, Clinton began to win back some of these voters to the Democratic Party but was unable to reverse the regime. Today, many of the formidable challenges in realigning this constituency with New Democracy remain. Reagan Democrats are especially susceptible to the patriotic appeals of the third corporate regime after 9/11. As immigrants or children of immigrants, they are drawn to the individualistic rags-to-riches stories that the regime propagates as part of the corporate mystique. They are socially conservative on issues such as gay marriage. And they still depend on corporations for their jobs; it is hard to bite the hand that feeds you.

Nonetheless, in the past decade, Reagan Democrats have become increasingly ripe for political realignment. The "deindustrialization of America"[7]—the devastating loss of jobs that manufacturing has suffered in the past twenty years—has hit the Reagan Democrats harder than it has any other major bloc of voters. The third corporate regime helped speed deindustrialization by its trade and tax policies. It added insult to injury by helping companies undermine unions and take back concessions on health, pension, and other benefits, while reducing government services many Reagan Democrats need.

A 2004 shift to the Democratic Party would be a first step in moving these voters toward regime change. Admittedly, this is no small task. As in all politics, the appeal of the message is not everything: much depends on the mes-

BLUE COLLARS COULD SWING THIS THING

Because the third corporate regime dealt them a bad hand, blue-collar workers are more receptive to a New Democracy agenda. New Democracy would help slow corporate flight, offer workers the jobs, workplace rights, and training they need, strengthen unions, and increase wages and benefits. The social security it would offer is vitally important to industrial workers. New Democracy would give the Reagan Democrats a fighting chance to win back the well-being and dignity that the New Deal helped them achieve a generation ago.

senger. A DLC Democratic president, such as Joseph Lieberman, is unlikely to inspire realignment. But Democrats with stronger populist messages could start the ball rolling. Over the past decade, regime-change Democrat Dennis Kucinich has been repeatedly reelected by blue-collar workers, including in one of the original homes of the Reagan Democrats, Parma, Ohio, a district that he carried by 74 percent in 2002. The victory prospects of a candidate such as John Kerry depend on his ability to connect with the voters of Parma.[8]

SUBURBANITES AND EXURBANITES: SOFTWARE GEEKS, SOCCER MOMS, AND OUTER-CITY MINORITIES

Hollywood movies like *Falling Down* (see "White-Collar Blues") speak to the angst of millions. Suburbs (the towns closest to the central city) and exurbs (the outer suburbs on the metropolitan fringe) have been traditionally seen as partisans of the corporate regime. Over the past two decades, however, they have experienced changes that might push them toward a new political alignment. The corporate regime is increasingly inflicting upon the white suburban population the same job and environmental traumas as it is Reagan Democrats and minorities in urban factories. The "software geek," a symbol of the white-collar, usually white suburban employee, whether in Silicon Valley or the high-tech suburbs around Boston, is seeing jobs sent to India, China, or the Philippines, where corporations such as Microsoft or Dell can hire highly educated

WHITE-COLLAR BLUES

In 1993, Warner Studios released *Falling Down*, a film that chronicled the life of a man on the edge. The protagonist, Bill Foster, masterfully played by Michael Douglas, exhibited the rage of a white, laid-off, suburban man who desperately tried but was unable to hold on to his suburban dream. One day, depressed over losing his job and furious about Los Angeles County traffic jams, Bill Foster left his car on the freeway and headed off on a killing spree.

". . . I am overeducated and underskilled
. . . I am not economically viable . . ."

BILL FOSTER, *a.k.a.*"D-Fens," *Michael*
Douglas's character in Falling Down

programmers, software engineers, or technicians and phone service center employees for far less money. More than a million white-collar jobs were outsourced in the 1990s, and Forrester Research estimates that 3.3 million more will disappear overseas by 2015. Ashok Deo Bardhan, a researcher on white-collar outsourcing, notes that 30,000 jobs were outsourced to India alone in June 2003, and that "14 million U.S. service jobs are vulnerable."[9]

Regime change may also be driven by the suburban soccer mom, who not only fears that her white-collar job could go overseas, but also is ensnared in traffic jams as she drives her kids to soccer games and has the added problem of bearing the costs of the corporate regime's slash-and-burn approach to child and family services. The spread of the social service crisis to the suburbs and the search for a low-growth environmentalism could lead suburban moms to support regime change to protect their families' quality of life.

The corporate regime is poised to undermine the white-collar economic base of the suburbs just as it already has the manufacturing base of the cities. The interests of Reagan Democrats in Flint would then align with interests of programmers in Silicon Valley. But does the Democratic tilt of the inner suburbs and, increasingly, the exurbs, suggest a shift in party and support for real regime change?

Granted, suburbanites are not likely to lead the charge for regime change. Suburban folks tilt toward individualism, privatism, and consumerism that the current regime offers. The growth of gated communities from Florida to California suggests that suburbanites have yet to reject the "Not in My Backyard" mentality that the regime encourages. And the regime rhetoric on taxes and race still play well to white suburbanites, many of whom left the city to avoid paying taxes that they perceived as supporting services for minorities. Moreover, "office-park dads," unlike their soccer mom wives, continue to lean heavily Republican, a gender gap that regime change politics will have to overcome.[10]

But if suburbanites won't lead the way toward progressive regime change, they are now less likely to resist it. They tend to be socially liberal, in favor of social services and environmental protections. Even the more conservative office-park dads want to reduce the deficit and increase spending on education, research and development.[11] The job security and broader economic interests of the white-collar suburban workforce now coincide more with New Democracy than with the global corporate regime. Almost 80 percent of white-collar workers share the view that corporations exercise too much influence on Washington,[12] and they could help propel a new suburban populism. Only regime change can create the global rules and social security that suburbanites increasingly need.

Changing demographics, job troubles, sprawl, and gender dynamics all propel traditionally Republican or Independent suburbanites in new directions. Inner suburbs have been voting more Democratic for some time; their growing percentages of African Americans and Latinos

Today's right-leaning exurb is
tomorrow's left-leaning suburb.[13]

RUY TEIXEIRA, *political analyst*

make them more like traditionally Democratic cities, as does the Democratic lean of suburban women. A 2003 poll showed that suburban moms favored Democrats over Republicans by 12 percent.[14] While rapidly growing exurbs have been touted by Republican analysts such as David Brooks as guaranteeing a Republican majority, Democratic analysts, including Ruy Teixeira and John Judis, have made a different case.[15] Teixeira shows that bellwether exurban counties, such as Virginia's Louden County, moved from 66 percent aligned with the GOP in 1988 to only 56 percent in 2000. Northern Virginia suburban and exurban counties as a whole moved "from a twenty-point advantage to a mere two-point advantage over that same period."[16] Similar trends have occurred in Maryland, Colorado, California, and around the nation, leading Teixeira to conclude that "as exurban counties become bigger, denser and more diverse, they generally become less—not more—Republican."[17]

RELIGIOUS VOTERS: FUNDAMENTALISTS, CHRISTIAN ACTIVISTS, AND SOCIAL JUSTICE WORKERS

In the 1970s, realignment came when Bible Belt Christian fundamentalists linked up with corporate activists to create the New Right and the Reagan Revolution. Ever since, the presumption has been that religious communities are unshakeable bulwarks of the current regime, and that the rise of religion as a more important force in politics and American life would inevitably boost neoconservative power blocs in Washington. But while fundamentalist religious activists in the South remain a key part of the Republican base, the neoconservative brand of politics is not representative of all fundamentalists.[18] Best-selling author and activist Jeremy Rifkin has shown that sectors of the fundamentalist Protestant community in the United States are committed to values that could help fuel a left-leaning political realignment.[19] Beyond these fundamentalists, there are millions of other religious activists and voters who could play a major role in a New Democracy regime change.

At Boston College, a Jesuit institution, several hundred activist students have joined me in the Global Justice Project I describe in Chapter 10, which is focused on the problems created by global corporations at home and abroad. I have been struck by how many of these activists are religiously inspired and see their faith as the foundation of their activist commitments. Many have come to their politics through Jesuit service programs in Central America, Appalachia, Native American reservations, or the inner city of Boston. Many graduate and go on to work in religious communities serving the poor or organizing workers at home or abroad. All of this reflects Catholic social doctrine and the voice of American Catholic bishops, who have played a role in promoting progressive change on issues such as nuclear war, poverty, a living wage, and broader forms of social justice. Papal encyclicals on work and social justice that date back

All economic life should be shaped by moral principles. Economic choices and institutions must be judged by how they protect or undermine the life and dignity of the human person, support the family, and serve the common good.[20]

at least a century and that were prioritized in the second Vatican Council, the historic meetings of Church leaders during the 1960s, helped inspire the bishops and lay out a vision of community economics, abolition of poverty, a living wage, workplace participation, and dignity for every worker and family.

The correspondence between the Catholic social vision and New Democracy is striking, explaining why so many Catholic students are now engaging in social justice activism, and why the Church could become a major force in a progressive regime change politics. The Voice of the Faithful, a grassroots group of lay Catholics responding to the priest sex abuse scandal, are seeking to democratize the Church itself. The group constitutes an advance guard of New Democracy that could mobilize the Church faithful toward a politics consistent with its social justice vision.[21]

Many of my own speaking invitations come from other churches. These include Unitarian Universalists, who do wonderful work across America and the world to advance economic justice and democracy, and Quakers, who are widely known for their institutional commitment to social justice and peace. Most of the mainline Protestant denominations have vibrant social justice branches serving the poor, feeding the hungry, and promoting policy changes from fair trade to environmental justice. Interfaith religious coalitions have been major players in promoting corporate responsibility and social investment. Anticorporate campaigns in the United States, whether against media monopolies, big tobacco, pharmaceuticals, or apparel giants, are increasingly led by coalitions of religious and labor groups. The National Labor Committee, a leading anti-sweatshop group that exposed the Kathy Lee Gifford/

Wal-Mart sweatshops in El Salvador, is a national coalition of religious leaders and unions that has organized global campaigns against Wal-Mart, Disney, Nike, and other corporations linked to sweatshops over the past decade.

Jewish religious groups who played a major role in the New Deal and more radical politics of the 1960s are raising their own voices against the regime. Despite the influential role of neoconservative Jews such as Paul Wolfowitz and Richard Perle in the Bush administration, and the increasing number of Jewish Republicans, many Jewish groups will be players in regime change politics. Rabbi Michael Lerner, editor of the Jewish magazine *Tikkun,* is an outstanding example. Lerner, a defender of Israel's right to exist with secure boundaries but also of a viable Palestinian state, speaks for hundreds of thousands of Jews who reject Wolfowitz's brand of neoconservatism, are horrifed by the foreign policy of the Bush administration, and vigorously oppose the Sharon government's brutal policies in the occupied territories. Emerging Jewish groups, such as Brit Tzdek V'Shalom, a Jewish organization for justice and peace, militantly oppose the neoconservative hawks and support a U.S. policy to create a contiguous, viable Palestinian state based on the pre-1968 borders. Jews continue to play a major role in the labor movement, civil rights movement (Lerner and African American leader Cornel West co-chair many common Jewish and African American political initiatives), labor unions, and other progressive groups.[22]

Religious groups rarely associated in the public mind with progressive politics—from Southern Baptists to Mormons to Muslims to Buddhists—support activists seeking social justice. This is hardly surprising since compassion,

WATCH OUT FOR THOSE NUNS

Religious activists can make quite a difference. According to Charles Kernaghan, a leader for worker rights around the world, no public protest more frightens managers at Niketown or Wal-Mart than a group of Catholic high school students with a few nuns.[23]

justice, and equality in the eyes of God are universal religious values. A regime change based on these values will inevitably draw the support of millions of deeply religious citizens.

THE BASE CAMP AND "AGGRESSIVE PROGRESSIVES": MINORITIES, WOMEN, LABOR, AND THE NEW SOCIAL MOVEMENTS

Realignment is vital to create regime change, but New Democracy's leadership and biggest groups will come from the historic progressive constituencies of the country. These groups were the heart of the New Deal, and they are now fired up to win significant social change in America. Their challenge is to unite with each other and mobilize support from disenchanted conservatives and the other people I have described. Progressives must also turn many of their own members from couch potatoes into active citizens.

The fall of the New Deal regime was precipitated by the fragmentation of the base camp into "special interest" groups focused on single issues, whether civil rights, abortion, higher wages, or gay rights.[24] Regime change requires bringing all these groups into a common network, with a vision broad enough to inspire the country as a whole.

People of color, especially African Americans and Latinos, are a key group because they are growing rapidly in number and their needs for regime change are intense. African Americans have been hardest hit by the corporate regime in almost every way. After the 2000 Florida vote debacle, which revived memories of the poll tax and other electoral disenfranchisement, they are mobilized not just to get Bush out but to help create a new kind of politics. Cedric Muhammed, the publisher of BlackElectorate .com, notes that "Black political and spiritual leaders [are] increasingly leaving the Democratic Party plantation" and speaking more forthrightly about the condition of the black community. Muhammed argues that blacks will abandon the Democratic Party in droves unless it shifts to a regime change politics for transforming the corporate order.

> Black leaders, and the Black electorate, are all candidates to embrace and borrow new ideas, policies and programs ... [because of] the worsening economic condition of Black America. The worse the situation becomes, the more likely a new paradigm will emerge with a critical mass to solve the problems that remain on the shelf, courtesy of failed and false leadership of bygone and current eras.[25]

Latinos share African Americans' need for an "aggressive progressive" paradigm. Poverty rates among Latinos run about 30 percent. The fastest growing minority vote in the country, Latinos tilt Democratic, traditionally about 70 percent in presidential elections. But beyond their need for a new economy, Latinos have special concerns; they are not only pro–affirmative action but also strongly pro-immigrant, and their political visions are heavily conditioned by 9/11.

The current regime's approach to terrorism may have already seriously destroyed its legitimacy among Latinos. Art Madrid, Republican mayor of La Mesa, California, for the past six years and a registered Republican for more than thirty years, says that the immigration policies of conservatives even before 9/11 were creating stresses, and that the Republicans have already lost the Latino community. "All they [the Republicans] can do is damage control now. They pulled the trigger before taking the gun out of the holster and shot themselves in the foot," Madrid said, referring to the punitive approach to immigrants. A conservative Latino, Nicholas Britto, former vice-chairman of the California Republican Hispanic Assembly, hits a raw nerve not just for Latinos but for other ethnic minorities: "For all the talk about family values, anti-immigration legislation is going to affect families, and that is one thing many ethnic groups will not tolerate," Britto says. "Don't forget, you don't have to scratch very far in the backgrounds of many people in this country before you find an immigrant."[26] Since the war on terrorism is the foundation of the current regime, the shift from social security to national security, and the anti-immigrant impulse in the new environment, could energize regime change politics among Latinos and other minorities.[27]

Women—a "majority minority"—share the urgent social security needs of African Americans, Latinos, and other minority communities. Though many women fear terrorist attacks (thus the slogan "Homeland Security Is for Girls"), they remain more strongly antiwar than are men. Political analyst Ruy Teixeira writes, "On virtually every poll question one might care to look at, women are less likely than men to trust and support Bush administration policies on Iraq and related issues, the main vehicle through which the president is supposedly fighting terrorist attacks."[28]

Corporations offer educated women economic opportunities, but it still is a glass ceiling regime, run at the top by an old boys' network. Female managers, blocked from moves to the top and unhappy with the "male dominance" ethos of the corporation, could become important players in regime change politics from the inside. Most women, whether in or out of the corporation, are threatened by the regime in unique ways. The regime is

curtailing reproductive choice and abortion rights
devastating child care and family support through
cutbacks in social services
downsizing and outsourcing clerical and other pink-collar
jobs
eroding part-time wages and security
undermining public education
stigmatizing and triaging single mothers.

The gender gap waxes and wanes, but it is a key force in American politics. Women remain far more committed than men to an activist- and social service–oriented government and to a society focused on nurturance rather than dominance. Moreover, women will never be full and equal players in the corporate regime despite its rhetoric of equal opportunity. The contradiction between the rhetoric and the realities for women, and the rise of large numbers of educated women committed to feminist ideals, will be a driving force behind regime change politics. A postcorporate regime will be feminist in spirit and power.

The third corporate regime is founded on the exploitation of workers across the planet, the majority of whom are female and nonwhite. A revitalized labor movement, both in the United States and abroad, is already rising to aggressively challenge the current regime. Labor was the most important group creating the New Deal regime and will lead regime change once again.

This seems counterintuitive, given the dramatic slide in the power of organized labor that has been orchestrated under the current regime. Less than 10 percent of private-sector workers are in unions, so union clout in the workplace and in Washington is eroding. Union members themselves, increasingly, vote independently of the Democratic-tilting labor leadership.

In the latter phases of the New Deal and in the Reagan years, many unions were narrowly focused on getting the best deal for their own members. Labor became just another "special interest" group with corrupt leaders. But the unrelenting assault on workers by the current regime has helped shift the identity of the labor movement. It increasingly sees itself as a social movement, recognizing that it can't win gains for its members unless it fights for all ordinary Americans. AFL-CIO leaders, including President

John Sweeney, have seen their main agenda over the past decade as organizing, organizing, and organizing, with the aim not just to increase union membership but to mobilize ordinary citizens to take back Washington from transnational corporations. In a September 18, 2003, speech for reelection as the AFL-CIO president, Sweeney signaled a new political approach.

> In this gilded era of global corporate greed, we have created a political program for the labor movement that is second to none—a model imitated across the political spectrum. We are changing the debate about trade and globalization, and we're building power for workers in the capital markets. We have created a vibrant new labor movement at the grassroots, helped unite the union movement to stand up for immigrant workers' rights, and brought thousands of young people into our efforts through Union Summer and campus outreach.[29]

While labor's shift toward a social movement is still evolving and is taking place largely under the public's radar screen, it is key to a corporate regime change. The politics of labor has changed dramatically since the end of the Cold War, with labor leaders no longer having to fear being called Communists if they speak up against U.S. foreign policy or for social justice at home. As global companies have recognized that they need to control Washington to survive, unions have come to the same correct conclusion. But since they cannot do so with money, the corporate tool, labor unions can do so only by winning the support of the people.

France provides a model. Americans are amazed when they see French citizens supporting strikes that disrupt their lives. But for the French people this is not a difficult decision: they see the labor movement as protecting their interests, not just those of union members. While only 10 percent of the French population is unionized, the labor movement leads successful social struggles for job security, fewer work hours, more public services, and other goals that benefit the whole population.

American unions are taking notice. John Sweeney's AFL-CIO has formed a new organization, Working America, for ordinary citizens who are not part of a union. Its aim is to promote "a social and political agenda for working-class people." Working America is modeled after the American Association of Retired People, "which collects dues to advance its platform for retired Americans."[30] This is one expression of Americans' new social movement unionism, akin to the French model, that seeks to promote social gains for all ordinary workers and citizens.

A multicultural labor movement is relatively recent, and it could be the recipe for regime change. New social movements—for the environment, peace, sexual equality, diversity, gay rights, and religiously inspired social justice—are already part of the American scene. But the melding of these movements with a labor movement fighting for regime change is something new. It just might be able to create what Americans most need and have least expected: regime change at home.

THE BIG TENT AND YOU

Can we really build a new big tent? Again, it all depends on you. Economic crises and cultural changes now make realignment and regime change possible. But only you can make it happen.

What can you do? Well, start by talking to family and friends who are hurt by the regime but do not yet see an alternative. Help educate them and open them to the idea of a regime change here in America. It's amazing how much change you can propel at a very personal level, partly because we are all so closely interconnected. We are all connected through a few links—six degrees of separation—to almost everyone else in the world. When you begin to educate and inspire your friends, you start a ripple that can spread quickly across global networks.

Begin with people who think along the lines as yourself. But to help build the big tent, try next to reach out to people who do not share your political views, whether they are family members or acquaintances at school, work, or church. If you are nonthreatening and informative, you may be surprised at the receptivity of people you never thought would agree with you about the dangers of corporate power in Washington and the need to shake up the political establishment.

But you can't do all the work alone. As I have said repeatedly, it will take organized movements of people to realign the political habits of Americans and rewrite the institutional rules of the game. In the Appendix, I summarize some personal change strategies and list organizations you can join to help create regime change at home.

APPENDIX
WHAT YOU CAN DO
TO PROMOTE
REGIME CHANGE

Before the elections:

1. Buttonhole a friend who is on the fence about Bush. Softly persuade or beat this person over the head until he or she agrees to vote against Bush and in favor of regime change at home.
2. Think of a friend who isn't going to vote. Persuade, trick, or bribe him or her to vote against Bush and promote regime change at home.
3. Send an email to every member of your family to tell them that you're disowning them if they don't vote against Bush and in favor of regime change.
4. Post flyers, cartoons, or charts, like those in this book, at your church, workplace, or gym.
5. Write your senators and reps or email the Democratic Party, and let them know that if they go Bush Lite, you'll abandon them.

After the elections:

1. If Bush wins, grieve for a week, remember my maxim "Embrace defeat," and then join one of the social movement groups discussed in this book.

2. If the Democrats win, celebrate for a week, remember my maxim "Think big and play offense," and join one of the social movement groups discussed in this book.
3. Whoever wins, join one of the organizations listed below.
4. Educate yourself about regime change by reading and joining discussion groups.
5. Educate others about regime change by sending them the books and articles that excited you.

You can't create regime change alone. But there's hope, because so many organizations are seeking to bring down the old pillars and build new ones. Here are the websites of a few of my favorites, organized by their focus on specific pillars:

Regime Change Organizations on Corporations and the Economy

NATIONAL LABOR COMMITTEE www.nlc.net.org
CENTER FOR STUDY OF RESPONSIVE LAW www.essential.org
PROGRAM ON CORPORATIONS, LAW, AND DEMOCRACY www.poclad.org
GLOBAL TRADE WATCH www.tradewatch.org
GLOBAL EXCHANGE www.globalexchange.org
FIFTY YEARS IS ENOUGH www.50years.org

Regime Change Organizations on Politics and New Democracy

TOMPAINE.COM www.tompaine.org
PUBLIC CITIZEN www.citizen.org
COMMON CAUSE www.commoncause.org
MOVEON.ORG www.moveon.org
ALLIANCE FOR DEMOCRACY www.thealliancefordemocracy.org

CAMPAIGN FOR AMERICA'S FUTURE www.ourfuture.org

RECLAIM DEMOCRACY www.reclaimdemocracy.org

Regime Change Organizations on Social Security and Social Justice

JOBS WITH JUSTICE www.jwj.org

AFL-CIO www.aflcio.org

PEOPLE FOR THE AMERICAN WAY www.pfaw.org

UNITED FOR A FAIR ECONOMY www.stw.org

ECONOMIC POLICY INSTITUTE www.epinet.org

CITIZENS FOR TAX JUSTICE www.ctj.org

UNITED STUDENTS AGAINST SWEATSHOPS
nate.clar47.rhno.columbia.edu/usas/about.html

SWEATX www.sweatx.net

Regime Change Organizations on a New Foreign Policy

OXFAM www.oxfamamerica.org

GREENPEACE www.greenpeaceusa.org

INSTITUTE FOR POLICY STUDIES www.ips-dc.org

BOSTON MOBILIZATION www.bostonmobilization.org

AMERICAN FRIENDS SERVICE ORGANIZATION www.afsc.org

UNITED FOR PEACE AND JUSTICE www.unitedforpeace.org

Regime Change Organizations on New Values and Citizen Empowerment

CENTER FOR A NEW AMERICAN DREAM www.newdream.org

FAIRNESS AND ACCURACY IN REPORTING www.fair.org

MAINSTREAM MEDIA PROJECT www.mainstream-media.net

GRASSROOTS SOLUTIONS www.grassrootssolutions.com

NOTES

Introduction

1. John Kerry, "Kerry Says U.S. Needs Its Own 'Regime Change,'" Glen Johnson, *The Boston Globe*, April 3, 2003.

2. I interviewed forty-seven workers between 1992 and 2003. I chose mostly to talk to temps, part-timers, freelancers, outsourced workers, etc., who have emerged as the new breed of workers in the current era. I taped the interviews, which lasted for about two hours each. Throughout this book I changed interviewees' names to protect their privacy. I conducted all the interviews in the Boston area, and I found the workers through temp agencies and personal references. These interviews provide not a scientific sample but simply a way to learn the stories of workers who are the new products of what I call today's "regime."

3. Charles Derber, *Corporation Nation* (New York: St. Martin's Press, 2000), Chapter 5.

4. This quotation, from the Progressive Party Platform, is cited in Theodore Roosevelt, *An Autobiography* (New York: DaCapo Press, 1998 [reprint]), Appendix B.

5. James Madison, "Monopolies, Perpetuities, Corporations, Ecclesiastical Endowments," Unpub-lished essay in collection of James Madison Papers, reel 26, series 2, volume 8, folio pages 2215–20. Cited online at http://www.sunnet works.net/~ggarman/estaorel.html.

6. For a list of such U.N. resolutions, see William Blum, *Rogue State* (Monroe, ME: Common Courage Press, 2000), 184ff.

7. Patrick Buchanan, *A Republic, Not an Empire* (New York: Regnery, 2002), and Kevin Phillips, *Wealth and Democracy* (New York: Broadway Books, 2003).

Chapter 1

1. Derber, *Corporation Nation*, 27.

2. Francis Fukuyama, *The End of History and the Last Man* (New York: Avon, 1993).

3. Matthew Josephson, *The Robber Barons* (New York: Harvest Books, 1962).

4. Harvey Wasserman, *Harvey Wasserman's History of the United States* (New York: Harper and Row, 1972), 74, 77.

5. Gabriel Kolko, *Main Currents in Modern American History* (New York: Pantheon Books, 1984), 3ff. See also Kolko, *The Triumph of Conservatism* (New York: Free

Press, 1977), and Martin Sklar, *The Corporate Reconstruction of Modern Capitalism* (Cambridge, Eng.: Cambridge University Press, 1995), for discussions of Theodore Roosevelt and the Progressive regime.

6. I have learned about Plan America from Elly Leary, a United Auto Workers official and labor historian, in personal conversations and from unpublished drafts of her work on the history of the labor movement.

7. Andrew Ross Sorkin, "$58 Billion Deal to Unite 2 Giants of U.S. Banking," *New York Times,* January 15, 2004.

8. Stan Cox, "Wal-Mart Gets Greedy," AlterNet, October 28, 2003, http://www.alternet.org/story.html?StoryID=17060.

9. Sarah Anderson and John Cavanaugh, *Field Guide to the Global Economy* (New York: New Press, 2000), 68.

10. The complete index can be seen at http://www.forbes.com/home_asia/2003/03/26/500sland.html.

11. Anderson and Cavanaugh, *Field Guide to the Global Economy*, 55.

12. Ibid.

13. Derber, *Corporation Nation,* 5ff.

14. Charles Derber, *People Before Profit* (New York: Picador, 2003), 61.

15. For the official biographies of the Bush administration cabinet, including the corporate histories of cabinet officials, go online to http://usinfo.state.gov/usa/infousa/politics/biograph.htm.

16. Eric Schlosser, "The Cow Jumped Over the USDA," *New York Times,* January 2, 2004.

17. Data on the Medicare overhaul bill and pharmaceutical spending can be found at the website of the Center for Responsive Politics (http://www.opensecrets.com), from figures compiled by Congressman Sherrod Brown (D, Ohio), and from posting of the watchdog group FAIR (Fairness and Accuracy in Reporting) at http://www.fair.org/activism/medicare-networks.html.

18. William Bridges, "The End of the Job," *Fortune,* September 19, 1994, 62. See also William Bridges, *Jobshift* (Boston: Addison Wesley, 1994).

19. Charles Derber, *The Wilding of America*, 3rd ed. (New York: W. H. Freeman/Worth, 2003), 93–94.

20. William A. Galston, "Perils of Pre-Emptive War," *The American Prospect* 13, no. 17 (September 23, 2002).

21. Richard Falk, *The Nation,* July 15, 2002.

22. Thomas Friedman, *The Lexus and the Olive Tree* (New York: Anchor, 2000), 104.

23. Ibid., xxi–xxii.

24. See Paul Krugman, *The Great Unraveling* (New York: Norton, 2003). See Krugman's discussion of how debt and deficits are used by the Bush administration as justification to "kill the beast," or to cut discretionary social spending to the bone.

25. For a comparison of inequality in the current corporate regime to inequality under earlier ones in the 1920s, and for a contrast with the picture during the New Deal, see Edward N. Wolff, *Top Heavy: A Study of the Increasing Inequality of Wealth in America* (New York: A Twentieth Century Fund Report, 1995). For more recent data, see Phillips, *Wealth and Democracy.*

26. Lynnley Browning, "After-Tax Income Gap Widening," *New York Times,* September 25, 2003.

27. Paul Krugman, "The Death of Horatio Alger," *The Nation,* December 23, 2003.

28. Ralph Nader, *Cutting Corporate Welfare* (New York: Seven Stories Press, 2000).

29. For discussion of these trends, see Krugman, *The Great Unraveling.*

30. For corporate constitutionalism at the WTO, see Derber, *People Before Profit.* See also Lori Wallach and Michelle Sforza, *The WTO* (New York: Seven Stories Press, 1999).

Chapter 2

1. William E. Leuchtenburg, *Franklin D. Roosevelt and the New Deal* (New York: Perennial Library, 1963), 44.

2. Ibid., 41

3. Ibid., 47.

4. For further elaboration, see Derber, *People Before Profit* and *Corporation Nation.*

5. Derber, *Corporation Nation,* 23.

6. Howard Zinn, *A People's History of the United States* (New York: Harper and Row, 1980), 367.

7. Wasserman, *History of the United States,* 31.

8. An anonymous worker in North Carolina, cited in Leuchtenburg, *Roosevelt and the New Deal,* 3.

Chapter 3

1. Thomas Kuhn, *The Structure of Scientific Revolutions* (Chicago: University of Chicago Press, 1996).

2. Ibid.

3. See Rick Pearlstein, *Before the Storm: Barry Goldwater and the Unmaking of the American Consensus* (New York: Hill and Wang, 2003), for a very similar analysis of Goldwater's impact on catalyzing the conservative movement.

4. Ted Nace, personal communication to the author, 2003.

5. Ibid.

6. I rely heavily on Ted Nace for this account of the corporate movement for regime change, which he calls "The Revolt of the Bosses." See Ted Nace, *Gangs of America* (San Francisco: Berrett-Koehler Publishers, 2003).

7. Ibid., 140.

8. Ibid., 142.

9. Ibid., 143ff.

10. Ibid., 142.

11. For an entertaining account of the rise of the New Right by an insider who eventually rejected the movement, see Michael Lind, *Up from Conservatism* (New York: Free Press, 1997). See also Robert Liebman, ed., *The New Christian Right* (New York: Aldine de Gruyter, 1983).

12. For a classic discussion of the grassroots protests that helped fuel the New Deal, see Richard Clowen and Frances Fox Piven, *Poor People's Movements* (New York: Vintage, 1979).

13. See Derber, *People Before Profit*, especially Chapter 9. See also Naomi Klein, *Fences and Windows* (New York: Picador, 2002).

14. Derber, *People Before Profit*.

15. Jim Hightower, *There's Nothing in the Middle of the Road But Yellow Stripes and Dead Armadillos* (New York: Harper Collins, 1998).

16. Jim Hightower, *Thieves in High Places* (New York: Viking, 2003).

17. See Alan Wolfe, *Rise and Fall of the Soviet Threat* (Boston: South End Press, 1980), for a discussion of how domestic credibility issues shaped U.S. politics during the Cold War.

18. Antonio Gramsci, *Selections from the Prison Notebooks* (New York: International Publishers, 1971).

19. See Lawrence Goodwyn, *Populist Moment* (New York: Oxford University Press, 1978).

20. William E. Leuchtenburg, *Roosevelt and the New Deal.*

Chapter 4

1. Raja Misra and Joanna Weiss, "Iraq Was Distraction, Clark Said," *The Boston Globe,* January 13, 2004.

2. Successive regimes have many forms of continuity as well as many differences, especially evident in foreign policy. Both the New Deal and Progressive regimes supported expansionist policies, and the corporate regimes that succeeded them continued and intensified those policies. This makes clear that regime change in the United States is not a revolution, and that certain capitalist tendencies, including expansionism, permeate all regimes.

3. This history of interventions

is drawn from Part III of Blum, *Rogue State*.

4. Noam Chomsky, *What Uncle Sam Really Wants* (Tucson, AZ: Odonian Press, 1991), 80.

5. Michael Moore, *Dude, Where's My Country?* (New York: Warner, 2003). See also Moore's film *Fahrenheit 911* due out in 2004.

6. Nicholas Leman, "The Next World Order," *The New Yorker*, April 1, 2002.

7. Ibid.

8. Ibid.

9. William Kristol and Donald Kagan, eds., *Rebuilding America's Defenses* (Washington, D.C.: Project for a New American Century, 2000).

10. "Defense Policy Guidance" (Washington, D.C.: U.S. Department of Defense, 1992).

11. Kristol and Kagan, *Rebuilding America's Defenses*, ii.

12. Stockwell made these comments on a publicly available tape recorded and played by the Public Broadcasting System. See also any of Stockwell's best-selling books, including *The Praetorian Guard* (Boston: South End Press, 1990).

13. The accounts in "Born to Intervene" are drawn from Blum, *Rogue State*, 49ff.

14. Amnesty International's report is posted online at http://web.amnesty.org/report 2003/index-eng.

15. Noam Chomsky, *Hegemony or Survival* (New York: Broadway, 2003).

16. Ibid. See also Noam Chomsky, *9-11* (New York: Seven Stories Press, 2001).

17. Rahul Mahajan, *Full Spectrum Dominance* (New York: Seven Stories Press, 2003), 167.

18. John Pilger, "This War Is a Fraud," Mirror.co.uk, May 21, 2002, http://www.mirror.co.uk/news/allnews/page.cfm?objected=11427607&method=full. See also John Pilger, *The New Rulers of the World* (London: Verso, 2002).

19. Mahajan, *Full Spectrum Dominance*, 167.

20. Ibid., 167–8.

21. Ibid., 167ff.

Chapter 5

1. Elizabeth Bumiller and Allison Mitchell, "GOP Betting on Homeland Security vs. Social Security at the Polls," *New York Times*, June 15, 2002.

2. Ibid.

3. Mark Gimein, "The Greedy Bunch," *Fortune*, September 2, 2002.

4. Paul Krugman, "Succeeding in Business," *New York Times*, July 7, 2002. See also Krugman, *The Great Unraveling*.

5. Bumiller and Mitchell, "Betting on Homeland Security."

6. Michael Bare, "Campaign 2004 II," April 23, 2003, http://www.mbare.org/archives/000096.html.

7. Steve High, "Who Knows How to Campaign?" Beating George Bush, July 30, 2003, http://beatinggeorgebush.blogspot.com/2003_07_01beatinggeorgebush_archive.html.

Chapter 6

1. "Bush Sought 'Way' to Invade Iraq?" *60 Minutes,* January 11, 2004, and posted on CBSNews.com, http://www.cbsnews.com/stories/2004/01/09/60minutes/main592330/.shtml/cmp=EM8707.

2. James Conachy, "US Troops Voice Anger at Pentagon," July 21, 2003, www.wsws.org/articles/2003/aug2003/sold-a07.shtml., 1, 2.

3. These lies are catalogued by James Vann, "Bush, 9-11, and Iraq—A Policy Founded on Deception," September 9, 2003, http://www.wsws.org/articles/2003/sep2003/bush-s09.shtml. For another extensive online cataloguing of these and other Bush lies, go to http://www.Bushwatch.com.

4. Daniel Benjamin and Steven Simon, "The Next Debate: Al Qaeda Link," *New York Times,* July 20, 2003.

5. Robert Dreyfus and Jason Vest, "The Lie Factory," *Mother Jones,* January/February 2004, 39.

6. Ibid.

7. Dreyfus and Vest, "The Lie Factory," 39, 41.

8. Ibid., 41.

9. Dana Milbank, "Bush Disavows Hussein–September 11 Link," *Washington Post,* September 18, 2003.

10. "Bush Backtrack on Saddam–911 Creates Legal Problem," http://www.theleftcoaster.com/archives/000563.html.

11. Sheldon Rampton and John C. Stanber coined the phrase "weapons of mass deception" with their eponymous book (New York: Tarcher, 2003). The lies I set forth are catalogued on many media and websites. For an overview citing these specific lies, see Fairness and Accuracy in Reporting, "Bush Uranium Lies the Tip of the Iceberg," July 18, 2003, http://www.fair.org/press-releases/beyond-niger.html.

12. See Dana Milbank, "For Bush, Facts Are Malleable," *Washington Post,* October 22, 2002, for a review of prior Bush misstatements on Iraq's nukes.

13. Vicki Allen, "Rumsfeld: We Saw Evidence in Dramatic New Light," Reuters, July 9, 2003, http://abcnews.go.com/sections/wnt/World/iraq030708_wmd.html.

14. Associated Press, "Kay Doubts Presence of Iraq Arms," ABC News, January 26, 2004,

posted online at http://www
.abcnews.go.com/wire/world/
ap20040126-235.html.

15. Mike Allen and Dana Priest,
"Bush Administration Is Focus of
Inquiry: CIA Agent's Identity Was
Leaked to Media," *Washington
Post,* September 28, 2003.

16. "Bush Welcomes Probe of
CIA Leak," CNN.com, October 1,
2003, www.cnn.com/2003/ALL
POLITICS/09/30/wilson.cia/.

17. How many U.S. soldiers
have been seriously wounded in
Iraq? You don't know, because the
U.S. military and the press are hid-
ing the numbers. NPR reporter
Daniel Zwerdling tried to get
the answer, but he only got the
runaround. After days of calling
military records officials, Zwerdling finally received an Army
confirmation that by December
2003, more than 8,848 soldiers in
the Army had been evacuated for
serious injuries. That doesn't count
the Marines, Air Force, or Navy,
and numbers grow every day.
Lieutenant Colonel Scott D. Ross,
of the U.S. military's Transportation Command, reported that he
had evacuated 3,255 battle-injured
casualties and 18,717 nonbattle
injuries. That is more than 21,000!
Republican Senator Chuck Hagel
of Nebraska, a Vietnam veteran,
has launched his own inquiry to
the Pentagon to come clean, since
there is such spotty and variable
reporting of these crucial numbers. See David H. Hackworth,
"Saddam in the Slammer," Soldiers
for the Truth, www.sftt.org/cgi-bin/
csNews/csNews.cgi?database=
Hacks%20Target.db&command=
viewone&op=t&id=49&rnd=240
.29326015816156.

18. Richard A. Oppel, Jr., "Con-
gressional Unit Analyzes Military
Costs in Iraq," *New York Times,*
November 1, 2003.

19. John Kifner, "Britain Tried
First. Iraq Was No Picnic Then,"
New York Times, July 20, 2003.

20. Ibid.

21. Antonia Juhasz, "Capitalism
Gone Wild," *Tikkun* 19, no. 1 (Jan-
uary/February 2004). All four of
these rules are detailed in this useful article.

22. "Cheney May Still Have
Halliburton Ties: Congressional
Report Finds Vice President Still
Has Financial Interest in Company," CNN.com, September 25,
2003, http://www.money.cnn.com/
2002/09/25/news/companies/
cheney/index.htm. On inflated oil
prices charged by Halliburton to
the U.S. armed forces, see Congressman Henry Waxman's statement on the floor of the House of
Representatives, "Contracting
Abuses in Iraq," October 15, 2003.

23. *The New York Times* first
reported this quotation from Chalabi, and it was later referred to in
numerous media, including CNN's

Crossfire, April 28, 2003, http://www.cnn.com/Transcripts/0311/28/cf.oo.html.

24. John Dean, "Missing Weapons of Mass Destruction: Is Lying about the Reason for War an Impeachable Offense?" FindLaw.com, June 6, 2003, http://writ.news.findlaw.com/dean/20030606.html.

Chapter 7

1. Steven Greenhouse, "U.S. Workers' Fears Rise as Job Losses Grow and Salaries Lag," *New York Times*, September 1, 2003.

2. I have drawn the four examples below from a collection compiled by minority members of the U.S. House Government Appropriations Committee, "The Photographic History of the Bush Administration Not Putting Its Money Where Its Mouth Is." David Sirota, minority contact, House Government Appropriations Committee, "The Bush Credibility Gap: Real Life Examples," July 25, 2003, www.house.gov/appropriations_democrats/caughtonfilm.htm. For additional examples, go online to the Bushwatch site at www.bushwatch.com/bushlies.htm, where I have verified some of these examples and added others.

3. Curtin is quoted on the House Government Appropria-

tions website, www.house.gov/appropriations.

4. Greenhouse, "U.S. Workers' Fears."

5. New York University economist Edward Wolff, cited in Andrew Lee, Robert Greenstein, and Isaac Shapiro, "A Reality Check on Recent Arguments in Favor of the Administration's New 'Economic Growth Plan,'" Center for Budget and Policy Priorities, January 28, 2003. For historical data, including shifts over the life of the current regime and comparison with earlier regimes, see Edward Wolff, *Top Heavy* (New York: Twentieth Century Fund Report, 1995).

6. These savings are detailed by Ralph Nader in a report from his Center for Responsive Law, 2003.

7. Robert Shapiro on CNN's *Crossfire,* and cited by Tax Policy Center, January 13, 2003, http://www.taxpolicycenter.org/news/bush_xfire.cfm.

8. Ibid., citing a Brookings Institute study.

9. William Gates, Sr., and Chuck Collins, *Wealth and Our Commonwealth* (Boston: Beacon Press, 2003).

10. Robert Greenstein and Joel Friedman, "Proposed 'Saving Incentives' Would Cause Revenue Hemorrhage in Future Decades," Center for Budget and Policy Priorities, March 6, 2003.

11. Ibid.

12. Grover Norquist, "Today, We Start Working for Ourselves," *National Review Magazine Online*, July 11, 2003, http://www.national review.com/nrof_comment/ comment-norquist071103.asp.

13. Garland Walker, "My Turn: Social Programs Under Attack," Juneauempire.com, http://www .juneauempire.com/stories/ 040703/opi_myturn1.shtml.

14. Edmund L. Andrews, "Leap in Deficit Instead of Fall Is Seen for U.S.," *New York Times*, August 26, 2003, http://www.globalpolicy .org/socecon/crisis/2003/0826 budget.htm.

15. Ibid.

16. The Treasury report is described online, "True Cost of Bush's Policies: $44 Trillion," May 29, 2003, www.dailykos.com/ archives/002850.html.

17. The story of the suppression of the administration's own $44 trillion deficit is described in Noam Chomsky, *Hegemony or Survival* (New York: Metropolitan Books, Harry Holt and Co., 2003), 119. Chomsky notes that the study is discussed in *The Financial Times* and *The Boston Globe*, and that press secretary Ari Fleischer agreed with the estimate.

18. Cited on http://budget .senate.gov/democratic/press/ 2003/ombmidsession2004brief analysis072303.pdf.

19. Paul Krugman, "Don't Look Down," *New York Times*, October 14, 2003. See also Krugman, *The Great Unraveling*.

20. Jeff Faux, "Rethinking the Global Political Economy," April 2003. Faux's speech is posted online at the Global Policy Network's website, http://www.gpn .org/faux-rethinking.html.

21. Ibid.

22. Krugman, "Don't Look Down."

Chapter 8

1. For a discussion of the 1917 and 1918 Sedition and Espionage Acts, see Howard Zinn, *A People's History of the United States*.

2. Ronald Brownstein, "Gore Urges Repeal of Patriot Act," *Los Angeles Times*, Novenber 10, 2003.

3. Greg Palast, *The Best Democracy Money Can Buy* (New York: Plume, 2003), Chapter 1.

4. "Fixing Democracy," *New York Times*, January 18, 2004.

5. "A Paper Trail for Voters," *New York Times*, December 8, 2003.

6. Palast, *The Best Democracy Money Can Buy*, a hard-hitting best-seller by an investigative reporter. See also Vincent Bugliosi, *The Betrayal of America* (New York: Thunder's Mouth Press/ Nation Books, 2001).

7. Gabriel Kolko calls this statist model "political capitalism," and he believes it began in the Progressive Era. See Kolko, *Triumph of Conservatism* and Derber, *Corporation Nation.*

8. Derber, *People Before Profit,* Chapter 3.

9. Derber, *People Before Profit.* See also William Greider, *One World Ready or Not* (New York: Simon and Schuster, 1998).

10. Giovanni Arrighi, *The Long Twentieth Century* (London: Verso, 1996).

11. Krugman, *The Great Unraveling.*

12. Scott Klinger, Chris Hartman, Sarah Anderson, John Cavanagh, and Holly Sklar, "Executive Excess, 2002: CEOs Cook the Books," (United for a Fair Economy), August 26, 2002.

13. Ibid.

14. Ibid., citing *Fortune,* September 2, 2002.

15. Michael Useem, *Investor Capitalism* (New York: Basic Books, 1999).

16. Ibid.

Chapter 9

1. Wasserman, *History of the United States,* 61.

2. Goodwyn, *Populist Moment,* vi.

3. Ibid., 71.

4. Ibid., 72.

5. Ibid., 47.

6. Ibid., 71ff.

7. Ibid.

8. This list is taken from http://www.shentel.net/sjc/links4.html, revised in December 2001 and accessed in January 2004.

9. I have learned much about BGAN from one of its founders and leaders, Mike Prokosch. For a discussion of the new "local to global" activist movements, see Mike Prokosch and Laura Raymond, eds., *The Global Activist's Manual: Local Ways to Change the World* (New York: Thunder's Mouth Press/Nation Books, 2002).

10. Personal communication from Noam Chomsky, 2003.

11. Adam Nagourney, "Political Strategies Changing," *New York Times,* September 1, 2003.

12. Ibid.

Chapter 10

1. Derber, *Corporation Nation,* 7.

2. John McCain, September 27, 1999, in Nashua, New Hampshire.

3. Theodore Roosevelt, "The New Nationalism," cited on http://www.fadedgiant.net/html/roosevelt_theodore_quotes.htm.

4. Cited on www.boston.com/dailyglobe/2/322/nation/British brace for Bush visit.shtml.

5. Joel Makower, *Beyond the Bottom Line* (New York: Simon and Schuster, 1994), 31.

6. Derber, *Corporation Nation.*

7. See the website for the Media Access Project, http://www.mediaaccess.org/programs/broadcastingoblig/.

8. For a review of these efforts, see Thom Hartmann, *Unequal Protection* (New York: Rodale, 2002).

9. Theodore Roosevelt, cited on http://www.fadedgiant.net/html/roosevelt_theodore_quotes.htm.

10. U.N. General Assembly Declaration of Human Rights, 1948. Article 23.3. This declaration was signed by the United States.

11. A summary of encyclical letters by the Pittsburgh diocese is given at http://www.diopitt.org/resource1.htm.

12. Patrick J. Buchanan, *A Republic, Not an Empire* (New York: Regnery, 2002).

13. George Washington's farewell address is posted on http://www.freedomwriter.com/issue23/am10.htm.

14. Dwight D. Eisenhower, Farewell Address, January 17, 1961.

15. Makower, *Beyond the Bottom Line*, 25.

Chapter 11

1. Richard L. Berke, "What You Say Can't Hurt You Until It Can," *New York Times*, November 9, 2003.

2. Keith T. Poole and Howard Rosenthal, *Congress* (New York:

Oxford, 1997) offers discussion of the history of realignments.

3. Howard Dean is quoted on the website Burnt Orange Report, http://www.burntorangereport.com/archives/cat_2004_presidential_election.html.

4. Ruy Teixeira, "Deciphering the Democrats' Debacle," *Washington Monthly*, May 2003, http://www.washingtonmonthly.com/features/2003/0305.teixeira.html.

5. Simon Romero, "U.S. Moves to Restrict Textiles from China," *New York Times*, November 19, 2003.

6. Pat Buchanan, "Press Releases," GoPatGo.com, December 15, 1999.

7. This term was coined by Barry Bluestone and Bennett Harrison in *The Deindustrialization of America* (New York: Basic Books, 1983).

8. Quoted from Dennis Kucinich's 2004 campaign website, http://www.kucinich.us/responses_1.htm.

9. Hiawatha Bray, "The White-Collar Migration—Part I," *The Boston Globe*, November 2, 2003.

10. Ibid.

11. Ibid.

12. Harris Poll, February 12–16, 2003, cited on www.kucinich.net/poll_support.htm.

13. Bray, "The White-Collar Migration—Part I."

14. Jill Lance, "Democrats Trying to Woo Suburban Dads," *USA*

Today, May 21, 2002. The poll was administered by Mark Penn, a moderate Democrat pollster.

15. Teixeira, "Democrats' Debacle." See also John B. Judis and Ruy Teixeira, *The Emerging Democratic Majority* (New York: Scribner, 2002).

16. Teixeira, "Democrats' Debacle."

17. Ibid.

18. Ed Kilgore, "Many Mansions: Churchgoers Don't Fit into Neat Pigeonholes," New Democrats Online, http://www.ndol.org/blueprint/2001_jul-aug/many_mansions.html.

19. Jeremy Rifkin, *The Emerging Order: God in the Age of Scarcity* (New York: Putnam, 1979).

20. National Conference of Catholic Bishops, *A Catholic Framework for Economic Life,* November 1996.

21. For an analysis of the Voice of the Faithful and its vision of democracy in the Church, as well as other Catholic canonical law related to social justice and democracy, see Derber, *Wilding of America,* especially Chapter 6.

22. See Michael Lerner, *Healing Israel/Palestine* (San Francisco: Tikkun Books, 2003) and *The Politics of Meaning* (New York: Putnam, 1997).

23. Charles Kernaghan, speech at Boston College, November 11, 2003.

24. Derber, *People Before Profit,* Chapter 9.

25. Cedric Muhammed, "The Black Electorate's Economic Vote," BlackElectorate.com, November 12, 2003, http://www.blackelectorate.com/articles.asp?ID=739.

26. Divina Infusino, "No Room in the Tent," Salon.com, http://www.salon.com/news/news960815.html.

27. Ibid.

28. Teixeira, "Democrats' Debacle."

29. Statement by AFL-CIO President John Sweeney Announcing ReElection Campaign, September 18, 2003, http://www.aflcio.org/mediacenter/prsptm/pr09182003.cfm.

30. Sarah Webster, "New Union Welcomes All," *Business News,* September 3, 2003, http://www.freep.com/money/business/aflcio3_20030903.htm.

INDEX

tion, 125; and domestic spending, 125; economic policies of, 158–71; and empire, 47; and environmental standards, 125; extremism of, 5, 26, 97–98; and financial scandals, 120–21; and fiscal responsibility, 168; and labor relations, 125; and normal or regime-change politics, 94; as threat to world peace, 219; personal taxes of, 163; rebranding of, 131, 163; reelection of, 9, 130–31; and regime change in Iraq, 6–7; relationship between terrorist enemy and, 103; and right-wing regime change, 70; social contract of, 45–46; and subsidies, 125; tax cuts of, 53–54, 125; trade policies of, 125; and "wag the dog," 128–29; and war at home, 45

Bush, Jeb, 177

Bush administration: "accomplishments" of, 125; and deficits, 52–53; extremism of, 11, 173–90; foreign policy of, 100–101, 103, 108–9; and global domination, 109–10; and privatization, 166; rhetoric of, 26; and weapons of mass destruction, 140–43

Bush Lite, 12, 13, 71

Bush Republicans, 10, 78

Business Council for Sustainable Energy, 87

Business Roundtable, 38, 86

Business Week, 187

Byrd, Robert, 211

Calgene, Inc., 38

California recall election, 178

California Republican Hispanic Assembly, 260

campaign contributions, 49, 55

campaign finance reform, 218, 226, 227

campus grassroots organizing, 206–8

capital gains tax, 163

capitalism, 31; corporations against, 182–84; and the third corporate regime, 184–90; undermining, 183–84

Carnegie, Andrew, 199

Carter, Jimmy, 63, 180

Caspian Basin oil reserves, 118, 119

Castro, Fidel, 23, 105

Catholic Church, 233

Catholic social doctrine, 255–56

Center for Budget and Policy Priorities, 165

Central America, 255; regime change in, 47, 56

CEO earnings, 187

Chalabi, Ahmad, 139, 153

Chao, Elaine, 38

Chase National Bank, 28

chemical weapons. *See* weapons of mass destruction.

Cheney, Richard, 37, 84, 112, 126, 138, 149; and Halliburton, 151; personal taxes of, 163; and weapons of mass destruction, 141

Chevron, 36

China, 251,

Chomsky, Noam, 108, 208, 243

Christian grassroots groups, 84

CIA, 106, 114; and connection between Iraq and 9/11, 137–39; covert intervention by, 105; information leak about, 143–44; and Valerie Plame, 143; and torture, 113–14; and weapons of mass destruction, 140

Citigroup, 28, 34, 35, 37, 127

civil liberties, 7, 69, 71, 173, 175–76, 236; ero-

sion of, 46; restraints on, 50

civil rights movement, 16, 68, 208

Civil War, 28, 34, 158, 174

Clark, General Wesley, 74, 94, 99

Clear Channel, 230

Cleveland, Grover, 13, 28, 66

Clinton, Bill, 13, 24, 27, 66, 74; and empire, 47; and Monica-gate, 121; and normal politics, 94; and Reagan Democrats, 249; social policies of, 45; status quo election of, 66–67

Cold War, 81, 103, 104, 235; as bad faith foreign policy, 104–8; as justification for repression, 108

collective security, 221–22, 234–35

Colombia, 115, 117, 118

Communism: as Reagan's enemy, 102, 105; war against, 107

Congressional Budget Office, 169

Connistraro, Vincent, 139

conservative populism, 88

conservatives, 245–48; grassroots, 248; social, 15; traditional, 15

constitutional rights of corporations, 225–27

consumerism, 50

Contract for America, 45

contract work, 43–44

Contras, 106

Control Data Corporation, 241

Coolidge, Calvin, 22, 30, 62, 65

Coors, Joseph, 86

corpocracy, 31–42, 185, 217; dismantling, 218

corporate abolitionism, 217–18, 237–38

corporate capitalism, 26

corporate charters, 223–25

corporate constitutionalism, 55–56

corporate elites, 4

206–8; and the Democratic Party, 212–14; global, 205–6; Internet, 202–5; and New Populists, 200–208; and Populists, 199–200

Great Britain: 1917 invasion of Iraq, 147–49, 152; and weapons of mass destruction, 142–43

Great Corporate Awakening, 63

Great Depression, 31, 42, 61, 92, 129

Great Society, 68

Greenberg, Stanley, 211, 212

Green Party, 213

Greenstein, Robert, 165

Grenada, 56, 107

Guatemala, 106, 107, 114

guerrilla war: during British occupation of Iraq, 148; in Iraq, 145

gun control, 15

Haas, Richard, 109–10

Haiti, 106, 107, 115

Halliburton, 37, 126, 149; and Richard Cheney, 151

Hamilton, Alexander, 24

Hamiltonian business regime, 27

Hardball, 129

Harding, Warren, 22, 27, 30, 66

Harken Energy, 37, 126

Harper, John, 86

Harrison, William Henry, 28

Havel, Vaclav, 138

Hayes, Rutherford B., 216

Head Start, 146

health care, 45, 54, 55, 58; costs of, 4; universal, 58, 81

Help America Vote Act, 178, 179

Heritage Foundation, 86

Hightower, Jim, 90, 159

HMOs, 41

Holding Company Act, 80

homeland security, 48, 129, 146, 175

Honduras, 106, 107, 114

Hong Kong, 34

Hoover, Herbert, 22, 27, 30, 31, 61, 62, 65, 80

Hooverism, 52

hope: and Franklin D. Roosevelt, 60; loss of, 9; prospects for, 241–43

HUD, 160

Humphrey, Derek, 2

Humphrey, Hubert, 68

Hussein, Saddam, 140; and 9/11, 136–37; as ally to U.S., 235; capture of, 131; Paul O'Neill on, 133; and regime change, 1; regime of, 23; U.S. aid to, 106

IBM, 35

ibn Ali, Hussein, 147

Ickes, Harold, 88

ideology: as a pillar of a regime, 25; of the third corporate regime, 33

immigrants, 248–51, 260–61

imperialism: American, 112, 148; global, 56

India, 147, 251

Indonesia, 106, 107, 118, 206

Institute for Global Communications, The, 204

International Atomic Energy Agency (IAEA), 141

International Criminal Court, 234, 236

International Monetary Fund, 207, 231

Internet, 82, 131–32; and grassroots organizing, 202–5; and regime change, 267–68; revolution, 89–90

intervention: in foreign countries, 106; unilateral, 112

investor capitalism, 188

Iran, 7, 21, 23, 118, 119, 152

Iran-Contra scandal, 104–5

Iraq, 21, 106, 107, 118; 1917 British invasion of,

147–49; 1958 coup in, 147; argument for invading, 110; Bremer orders on, 150; connection between 9/11 and, 136–40; cost of war in and occupation of, 146–47; as a crisis for the Bush administration, 133–55; elections in, 136; end of "major hostilities" in, 130; foreign investment in, 150; and oil, 121; preemptive invasion of, 47–48; president's lies and distortions regarding, 134; protests against war in, 7–8; regime change in, 7; trade liberalization in, 150; U.S. sanctions on, 120; and weapons of mass destruction, 40–43

Iraq exit strategy, 144–47

Iraqi National Congress, 139

Iraqi perfect storm, 133–55

Iraq occupation: attacks on U.S. troops during, 145–46

Iraq war, 6, 9, 45, 56; argument for, 110; cost of, 146–47; end of "major hostilities" of, 130; possible democratic outcomes of, 152–53; protests against, 7–8; and weapons of mass destruction, 140–43

Israel, 117, 120, 257

Janitors for Justice, 172, 208

Jefferson, Thomas, 240, 247, 225

Jeffersonian Republicanism, 27

Jewish Republicans, 257

jobs: loss of, 42–44, 52, 159, 161, 167, 249; movement overseas of, 76, 251–52; temporary, 182–83

Johnson, Lyndon B., 68, 75, 135–36, 233

ABOUT THE AUTHOR

Charles Derber is Professor of Sociology at Boston College and former director of its graduate program on Social Economy and Social Justice. Derber received his undergraduate degree at Yale University and his PhD at the University of Chicago. He is a scholar in the field of political economy, international relations, and society, with eight internationally acclaimed books and major research grants from the U.S. Department of Education and the National Institutes of Mental Health.

Derber's books have been reviewed by *The New York Times, The Washington Post, The Boston Globe, The Boston Herald, The Washington Monthly,* and other publications. His op-eds and essays appear in *Newsday, The Boston Globe,* and *Tikkun,* and he is interviewed frequently by *Newsweek, Business Week, Time, Bloomberg,* and *The L.A. Times* for stories about business and politics.

Derber has addressed the Council on Foreign Relations, the Conference Board, the Council on Philanthropy, and other policy institutes. He speaks at universities in the United States and abroad and has given keynote addresses to the national Unitarian Universalists, the New England Sociological Association, and many university groups.

Derber is an outspoken advocate for social change, working closely with many grassroots movements focused on peace and social justice. He organized a worker education program with the United Auto Workers and worked with eight unions on problems of displaced workers. He recently returned from a book tour of Germany, Austria, and Italy, organized by the European antiglobalization organization, AT-TAC, and the Italian Active Citizens Network. Derber is married and lives in Dedham, Massachusetts.

Berrett-Koehler Publishers

Berrett-Koehler is an independent publisher of books and other publications at the leading edge of new thinking and innovative practice on work, business, management, leadership, stewardship, career development, human resources, entrepreneurship, and global sustainability.

Since the company's founding in 1992, we have been committed to creating a world that works for all by publishing books that help us to integrate our values with our work and work lives, and to create more humane and effective organizations.

We have chosen to focus on the areas of work, business, and organizations, because these are central elements in many people's lives today. Furthermore, the work world is going through tumultuous changes, from the decline of job security to the rise of new structures for organizing people and work. We believe that change is needed at all levels—individual, organizational, community, and global—and our publications address each of these levels.

To find out about our new books,
special offers,
free excerpts,
and much more,
subscribe to our free monthly eNewsletter at

www.bkconnection.com

Please see next pages for other books
from Berrett-Koehler Publishers

Alternatives to Economic Globalization
A Better World Is Possible
2nd Edition, updated and expanded (10/04)

John Cavanagh and Jerry Mander, Editors

Alternatives to Economic Globalization is the culmination of a three-year project to define alternatives to the current corporate model of globalization. This official consensus report of the International Forum on Globalization lays out alternatives to the corporate globalization more fully, specifically, and thoughtfully than has ever been done before.

Paperback • ISBN 1-57675-303-4
Item #53034 $18.95

America As Empire
Global Leader or Rogue Power?

Jim Garrison

Jim Garrison asserts that America has transitioned from republic to empire and urges all Americans to face up to the complexities and responsibilities inherent in that fact. He calls on Americans to consciously see their country as a transitional empire, one whose task is not to dominate but to render the need for empire obsolete.

Hardcover • ISBN 1-57675-281-X • Item #5281X $24.95

Gangs of America The Rise of Corporate Power and the Disabling of Democracy

Ted Nace

Gangs of America details the rise of corporate power in America. Driven to answer the central question of how corporations got more rights than people, Ted Nace delves deep into the origins of this institution that has become a hallmark of the modern age. He synthesizes the latest research with a compelling historical narrative to tell the rich tale of the rise of corporate power in America.

Hardcover • ISBN 1-57675-260-7 • Item #52607 $24.95

Berrett-Koehler Publishers
PO Box 565, Williston, VT 05495-9900
Call toll-free! **800-929-2929** 7 am-9 pm EST

Or fax your order to 1-802-864-7626
For fastest service order online: **www.bkconnection.com**

Spread the word!

Berrett-Koehler books are available at quantity discounts for orders of 10 or more copies.

Regime Change Begins At Home
Freeing America from Corporate Rule

Charles Derber

Hardcover
ISBN 1-57675-292-5
Item #52925 $19.95

To find out about discounts for orders of 10 or more copies for individuals, corporations, institutions, and organizations, please call us toll-free at (800) 929-2929.

To find out about our discount programs for resellers, please contact our Special Sales department at (415) 288-0260; Fax: (415) 362-2512. Or email us at bkpub@bkpub.com.

Subscribe to our free e-newsletter!

To find out about what's happening at Berrett-Koehler and to receive announcements of our new books, special offers, free excerpts, and much more, subscribe to our free monthly e-newsletter at www.bkconnection.com.

Berrett-Koehler Publishers
PO Box 565, Williston, VT 05495-9900
Call toll-free! **800-929-2929** 7 am-9 pm EST

Or fax your order to 1-802-864-7626
For fastest service order online: **www.bkconnection.com**